The Call
A Journey into Men's Ministry

Endorsements

It's sometimes amazing what God will do to get your attention to move into the place HE wants you. I have known Mike for a few years now, working with him through Iron Sharpens Iron. Finally, Mike is where he is supposed to be building men. In this book, Mike shares his life's journey and tools you can follow that will help you build men in your church.

Rex Tignor
Man-Up Ministries
Iron Sharpens Iron

Mike Sandlin's story, his journey, and his counsel are invaluable to any man who is ready to put into practice the (great) commission of Jesus Christ to go into all (your) world and make disciples. Listen to Mike. Learn from Mike. Follow Mike as he follows Jesus.

Rev. Marty Granger
Founder and President
Ministry Alliance

The Calling to Minister to Men is the missing link the church has been awaiting. My friend, Mike Sandlin, has weaved his personal story into a practical plan that will be a great resource for effective men's ministry. I'm personally buying copies for every men's leader I know.

Dr. Mark Denison
Founder
There's Still Hope

Mike Sandlin has a great heart for men and a burden to help men become dedicated followers of Jesus. Mike understands that there are unique challenges that men have in their lives, and in his book, *The Call: A Journey into Men's Ministry*, Mike offers practical ideas on how to help the men of your church grow to be disciples of Jesus in all aspects of their lives.

Richard Brunson
Director
North Carolina Baptists on Mission

In a field that has consistently proven to be a challenge for the local church, Mike Sandlin provides encouragement and practical advice on how to minister to men with intention. His passion comes from life-changing experiences; Mike stands shoulder to shoulder with men's leaders, exhorting them to remain faithful to the call. *The Call: A Journey into Men's Ministry* is an important read for anyone who cares about making a true difference in the lives of the men around them.

Mark Abernathy
Consultant for Men's Ministry
North Carolina Baptists on Mission

Over the past 20 years, it has been fascinating to watch the transformation of Mike Sandlin from a businessman who "had a yearning" to help men find the fullness of life in Jesus Christ to a man who is "fully engaged and fully occupied" in the quest to help men. It has been instructional to me to see how God brings to fruition that which he calls a man to do. Mike is a man skilled and passionate about his calling, and it is certainly worthwhile to read his new book: *The Call: A Journey into Men's Ministry.* I thank God for men like Mike Sandlin.

Nathan Sanders
Businessman

The Apostle Paul encouraged Timothy to "teach these truths to other trustworthy people who will be able to pass them on to others" (2 Timothy 2:2). Mike lives out this admonition in his life as evidenced by his passion for Jesus and his desire to see churches equip men to be devoted disciples of Jesus. This book can help you do the same.

Willie Batson
Author/Speaker/Pastor
WC Batson Consulting

I heartily recommend the book to you. If you are blessed to know Mike, you will better understand his passion. If you haven't yet met Mike, you will see why he is passionate about ministering to men. This book will inspire and educate the need to reach men and give many helpful insights into how to have a fruitful ministry to men in any size or type of church. The issues Mike writes about have true eternal significance.

Roy A. Smith
Associational/Network Missions Strategist
Cape Fear Network of Baptist Churches

In a winsome style, Mike Sandlin shares his own story of how God used multiple men to build into his life. He then shares some principles and tips so that you and I can do the same. He reminds us over and over that when we build godly men - everyone wins!

Brian Doyle, Founder and President
Iron Sharpens Iron

Read through these pages and you'll hear the voice of experience, you'll sense the assurance of a calling and you'll feel the depth of passion that have made Mike Sandlin a trusted advisor to many pastors and leaders for years. You'll enjoy his real-world stories and practical tips. Whether you're brand new at men's discipleship or an old pro looking for fresh ideas, you will find them here!

Brett Clemmer
President/CEO
Man in the Mirror

The Call
A Journey into Men's Ministry

by
Mike Sandlin

The Call
A Journey Into Men's Ministry

ISBN: 978-1-7359739-9-9

Copyright © 2021 by Mike Sandlin

ALL RIGHTS RESERVED. *No part of this book may be reproduced in any form without permission in writing from the publisher, except in the case of brief quotations embodied in critical reviews or articles.*

All scriptures are from English Standard Version (ESV) unless noted.

Printed in the United States of America
2021 -- First Edition

Published by Austin Brothers Publishing

Fort Worth, Texas

*This book is dedicated to my Bride Joanne,
who has been by my side in sickness and health,
for richer or poorer, good times and bad.*

Love You, Babe!

Acknowledgments

This book would not have been possible without the number of people who pushed me and provided mentorship and encouragement.

Much of what is written in this book results from the teaching and encouragement from my mentor Jeff (Coach K) Kisiah, who went home to be with the Lord on May 3, 2019. He helped me understand how to reach into men's lives for the glory of God.

Other mentors include the Rev. Roy Smith, who I met with monthly as he poured into my life to formulate the ministry to men and serves as a ministry advisor for Cape Fear Men; Nathan Sanders, a good friend and ministry advisor who has always encouraged me to pursue the things for which God has given me a passion; Gary Davis, who I consider one of my best friends, who provided insight and editorial comments as this book was being developed; Rex Tignor, who encouraged me to write this book and provided review comments as I wrote my first draft; and Mark Denison, who served as my mentor in getting this book published.

Most of all, to my wife, who has always been by my side: spending hours with me in the hospital dealing with procedures and surgery, never leaving once I was admitted to the hospital until I was discharged—and being my Bride for 46 years. I cannot leave out my children, who have given me such a blessing as I have watched them grow into a mighty man of God and a mighty woman of God. God blessed them with spouses who serve God and two grandchildren who have captured my heart in more ways than one can count.

And to my Lord and Savior Jesus Christ, who has given me the passion and burden to reach men for His kingdom.

Contents

Introduction	1
God Used a Kidney Stone	3
The Calling	17
Just Because	35
Leading Your Men	53
Discipling	71
Invite Someone to Take a Journey	91
How To Get Men Involved	105
Keep the Fire Burning	123
Epilogue	137
The Roman Road	141
Barnabas Lunch Appointments	143
Example of a Simple Survey	147
Resources	151
Endnotes	153
About the Author: Mike Sandlin	156

Introduction

When God captured my heart for men's ministry, I recognized there is as much work to do within the church as there is outside the church.

Up to this point, my involvement in ministering to men was attending breakfast meetings, an occasional men's conference, and periodically participating in mission opportunities. Never did I understand, nor did I see it demonstrated that ministering to men was much more. A truly effective and vibrant ministry to men focuses more on moving men into discipling relationships.

The men's ministry I had been involved with most of my church life was nothing more than a social gathering. Though gatherings are needed and are required, the purpose of those gatherings should be to give men the next right step toward a discipling relationship. However, when I began ministering to men, I

The Call

did not know where to start, like many who start in men's ministry. Eventually, God brought men into my life to mentor and guide me in this new adventure.

I pray as you read the story of how I began ministering to men, the ideas and insights I will share, and my experiences in will inspire you to move the men of your church in such a way they will grow in Christ. As you allow God to work through you, I hope this book will be a source to help you understand areas to focus on to have a vibrant and effective ministry to men in your church.

A Journey Into Men's Ministry

Chapter 1
God Used a Kidney Stone

We know that for those who love God all things work together for good, for those who are called according to his purpose.
Romans 8:28

The Day Began Like Any Other

It was December 22, 2006. I was on a two-week vacation from work and hanging out at the house. I had been sore in my groin area the past week, but I felt better this morning—no discom-

The Call

fort at all. My wife was at work on her job as the Clinical Nurse Manager at a local physician's office.

A couple of days earlier, she made an appointment with one of the doctors in the office to investigate the reason for the soreness. My appointment was at 9:00 am. Not long after arriving at her office, she called to check on me.

When the phone rang, I could tell from the caller ID it was probably her calling.

"Hello."

"How are you feeling this morning?" Joanne said.

"I feel pretty good," I said.

"You coming in for the appointment?"

"I'm actually feeling good—no soreness at all. I don't think I need to see a doctor. Why don't you cancel my appointment and give it to someone who really needs to see the doctor?" I told Joanne with a little bounce in my voice.

> *Just three days before we were to leave with 43 others, mostly high school students, I had my first kidney stone attack in 1995.*

"You sure?"

"Yeh. I probably just pulled something, and it has finally worked itself out. I'm okay." Then I added that proverbial phrase all men say, "I'm fine."

Joanne said, "Okay." I could tell in her voice she disagreed with me about canceling the appointment but went along.

After saying our goodbyes, I returned to work on my computer while sitting at my desk in our home office.

Excruciating Pain

It was not thirty minutes later when I was hit with an excruciating pain in my back that radiated around to the front and into the groin. It doubled me over. After a few minutes, the pain eased off, and I almost felt normal. I started moving a little like one does when they have pulled a muscle to work it out. Then suddenly, there it was again. Excruciating. It was then I realized, and I knew without a doubt what was causing the pain—a kidney stone. Once you have one, you will never forget the pain. They say it is the closest thing a man can experience to a woman giving birth. If that is true, I do not know how women can do that over and over again. No wonder they scream while giving birth, "This is YOUR fault!"

Just three days before we were to leave with 43 others, mostly high school students, I had my first kidney stone attack in 1995. We were heading to Bagley, Minnesota, to conduct Vacation Bible School on an Indian Reservation and at a couple of Bagley churches. We were scheduled to be gone for two weeks.

It was Sunday morning, and we were in church. I was a little uncomfortable during Sunday School, and I stepped outside the class to see if I could relax. I did begin to feel better, and we went on to the church service. I served as an usher that morning, so I was in the vestibule with a few other men when I started with

The Call

the uncomfortableness again. This time the pain continued to increase.

The men serving with me began to realize something was wrong and started asking if I was okay. I finally told them to get Joanne; I needed to go home. So someone went to get Joanne, and another went to get our children elsewhere in the building. They helped me out to the parking lot and into our van about the time our children arrived.

Joanne said we are going to the hospital, but first, we would go by the house and let our children stay there. I don't remember if we had someone come over and stay with them since Matt was 15 and Shelley was 11 years old. All I cared about was getting to the hospital.

As my wife was driving me to the hospital, she stopped at every red light and drove the speed limit. Which, by the way, is what she should be doing. But I was screaming at her, "WHY ARE YOU STOPPING?!?!" "Why are you going so slow?!?!"

With her being a nurse, she had a good idea of what was wrong. Instead of being all sympathetic, she sat over there, all comfy in her seat, almost laughing at me. Actually, I think she was, as I thought I saw her eat a smile.

Now, here we are, eleven years later, and the pain has returned. It was the same pain I felt those eleven years earlier. Something must be done!

Off To The Office

Thinking like a man in extreme pain, I did what any man would do; I grabbed my keys, jumped into my truck, and started to Joanne's office. As I was driving, I did another smart thing. I picked up my cell phone and called Joanne and told her I was coming in.

"I know what is wrong!" I said when she answered.

"What?" came the reply on the other end of the phone.

"A kidney stone!" I cried.

With God's protection, I arrived at the office safely. I came in through the back door, the one reserved for employees. I mean, my wife is the manager; shouldn't that give me some perks? Then again, she told me to come in that way.

I went straight to her office. She took one look at me and took me straight to an exam room. She went and got Dr. Jones, who came in, did a quick examination, and ordered a CT scan. She was also kind enough to order a shot of some pain-relieving medication to relieve the pain. Boy, did that feel good.

However, we had to go to another office for the CT scan. Joanne took me. Dr. Jones had her nurse call ahead, and they were waiting for us when we arrived and took me straight back to the exam room. After completing the scan, they sent me to the lobby while reviewing the scans to ensure the pictures were clear enough for the doctor. After several minutes of waiting, I started to get uncomfortable again, so Joanne decided we would head

The Call

back to her office. They would call Dr. Jones and let her know the results.

When we arrived at Joanne's office, the radiologist had already called Dr. Jones with the results. She told us I had a stone in my left kidney. But that was not the only thing they saw. It seems I have a 4-centimeter tumor on my right kidney—the size of a golf ball. I needed further examination, and I needed to see a urologist as soon as possible. No kidding. I wasn't concerned about the tumor. That was not the problem. It was that stone reminding me, again and again, it was there.

She told us I might be able to pass the stone. After prescribing Percocet to take for the pain, she sent me home, telling us to call if I had any problems over the weekend. We were three days from Christmas of 2006, and Christmas was on a Monday. It was going to be a long weekend and a Christmas to remember.

I suffered through the Christmas weekend, taking Percocet every so often as the pain came. I never liked taking narcotics to relieve pain. However, I can promise you that if I took one, I was indeed in pain. As the weekend wore on, I was not having any success with passing the stone.

I remember sitting in one of our comfy chairs over away from most of the family at our house on Christmas day. Joanne's mom, and brothers and sister with their families were there. In all, there were seventeen roaming around our house that day. Everyone knew I had a kidney stone, but no one—including our children—knew about the tumor.

A Journey Into Men's Ministry

Heading to the Hospital

Tuesday morning came with no relief. Joanne took me in with her to the office, and we talked with Dr. Jones. After Dr. Jones spoke with a urologist, she sent us to the Emergency Room at New Hanover Regional Medical Center, where the urologist on call that day met us. God watched over us as this man was a down-to-earth doctor who had time to explain all that was going on.

At the Emergency Room, they prepped me to remove the stone. They wheeled me back to start the procedure. After administering anesthesia to put me to sleep for the procedure, I knew nothing until I woke up in the Recovery Room. I learned there had been complications, and I was not going home—I was being admitted to the hospital.

Once I was moved to my room, Joanne was there, and she told me what had happened. During the procedure, the ureter, the tube that connects the kidney to the bladder, acquired a hole from the laser used to break up the stone. So now I was passing urine into my abdomen. The doctor had tried to place a stent in the ureter while in surgery but was unsuccessful. I felt fine as long as I laid still, but when I tried to sit up, which caused the abdomen to compress, the pain was tremendous as my body was trying to squeeze all that fluid.

Most people probably think the urine leaking into the body cavity would be poisonous, but it is not. Urine is sterile until it mixes with the air outside the body. So as long as it was within

The Call

the confines of my body, I was okay. It was just uncomfortable because the urine was where it was not supposed to be.

The doctor scheduled an intervention radiological procedure to insert a tube in my back, penetrating the kidney, then routing the tube through the ureter and into the bladder to seal the hole in the ureter. This would allow the ureter to heal. The doctor tried three times to punch a hole into a deflated kidney while I was in the hospital. He explained it was like trying to punch a hole in a deflated balloon. Try it. All the balloon will want to do is move around unless you can hold it down. Well, you cannot hold the kidney to keep it from moving. So each time they tried, the kidney just pushed away.

Let me tell you, laying on that procedural table on my stomach was no picnic. Before starting the procedure, the doctor prepared me for what was going to happen. Using an x-ray, they would determine where to insert the needle with the tube and guide it through the kidney and into the ureter. The kicker: They could not use any anesthesia for the process, so I would feel him pushing the needle into my back. Yeah... it hurt. It hurt real bad.

I felt sorry for the nurse who was sitting at my head, holding my hands. Whenever they would push the needle into my back, I would squeeze her hands because of the pain. I was afraid each time that I would break her hands.

> *"We must repair the damage to the left kidney before we could do anything with the right."*

After a few tries over the next few days, they successfully got a tube in to drain the urine from my kidney, preventing it from leaking into my body cavity. Though I did not have the tube to allow the ureter to heal, they decided to let me go home and bring me back in a few days to try again. I went home with a nephrostomy bag strapped to my leg after being in the hospital from Tuesday through Friday during the last week of December 2006.

What's Happening to Me?

Over the next few days after arriving home, I began to understand my situation. I have a tumor on my right kidney, and the damage to the left ureter prevented the left kidney from draining properly. Before leaving the hospital, the urologist told us, "We must repair the damage to the left kidney before we could do anything with the right."

Up to this point, I was walking through a denial mindset that I may have cancer. After arriving home, I woke up one morning, and Joanne was helping me out of bed. She had just helped me put my feet on the floor and was getting ready to help me stand when it finally hit me. All my emotions started welling up, and I could no longer control them. I just reached out and grabbed her, holding her close to me, and I began to bawl like a baby. I could not stop for several minutes.

Through this, I began to question why God was allowing this to happen. I was still a young man in my eyes—only 52 years old. I did not have any grandchildren to enjoy as my children were not married. I had so much I still wanted to do. All I could think of is that I have cancer—or so it appears—so how much more time did I have?

Then God reminded me of my favorite verse, a verse that had quickly become a favorite of mine almost from the first time I heard it. "All things work together for good to those who love God and are called according to His purpose," Romans 8:28.

All things. No matter if they are good or bad. And this was a bad thing. So God, how are You going to work this to good? He would show me in a matter of weeks.

Back to the Hospital

A few days later, I was back in the hospital as an out-patient for another Intervention Radiological procedure to insert the tube to allow the ureter to heal. The procedure allowed me to shed the nephrostomy bag strapped to my leg for the past week. I would have this tube in me for approximately ten weeks.

It was uncomfortable to walk, as the other end was in my bladder, and I could feel it with each step I took. I could not walk many steps without stopping and allowing my body to recover from the rubbing I felt.

Over the next ten weeks, I visited the doctors at the University of North Carolina Memorial Hospital in preparation for the surgery. We learned I was going to lose my right kidney. The tumor was located at the entrance of the major blood vessels into the kidney, and to obtain clear margins, it would require cutting into those vessels.

The doctors assured me living with one kidney is not a concern; many go through life with one kidney. I did not realize this until I was the one losing a kidney. God helped me understand this is not as bad as it seemed as He began to put people in my life who are living with one kidney and living a very healthy and productive life. He even put a man in my life working as a personal trainer at the gym where Joanne and I were members, who was born with one kidney. It is amazing how God will provide encouragement during our time of difficulty.

I began to feel more comfortable

> *But the real story is what God has been doing in my life and heart since discovering the tumor. In the rest of the book...*

with my long-term prognosis. The only unknown was if the tumor was truly cancerous and if it would potentially spread. Because of the location and the type of tumor, the doctors could not do a biopsy, so we would not know for sure until the tumor was removed and examined.

Ten weeks after having the tube inserted to allow the ureter to heal, I was back in the Intervention Radiological Unit to have the tube removed and examine the damaged area. After determining the ureter was healed, the doctors removed the tube from my body. When I got up from the table, I felt like a new man as I could walk with no discomfort. That part of my journey was over. Now on to the surgery to remove the tumor and kidney.

The Call

The Story Is Just Beginning

Three months after the tumor was discovered, I went into surgery on March 23, 2007, and the surgeon removed the tumor along with the kidney. Pathology later reported the tumor was Renal Cell Carcinoma, more commonly known as Kidney Cancer. The good news was the cancerous tumor was encapsulated, and there was no indication of a spread.

As I write this, it has been fourteen years since removing the tumor, and now I am considered cured.

But the real story is what God has been doing in my life and heart since discovering the tumor. In the rest of the book, you will discover how God spoke to me about ministering to men and the things we need to be aware of as we reach into men's lives.

A Lesson on How God Prepares Us for Future Events

God prepares us for the future through events in our life. Four years later, almost to the day of my kidney stone attack and discovery of the tumor, our daughter Shelley had a kidney stone attack. When they CT scanned her, they discovered a tumor on one of her kidneys. Hers was not as large, and she did not lose the kidney, but the message was clear that God prepared her for her cancer journey through my cancer journey.

As she watched her dad go through the process, she knew she could and would recover. She is now ten years removed from the original diagnosis and is considered cured. Once again, Romans 8:28 came alive for her and me.

"All things work together for good to those who love God and are called according to His purpose."

The Call

Questions to reflect on for your next step.

- What has occurred in your life that you can see God using to get your attention?

- Has there been an event in your life that some may see as bad, but God meant for good? Explain

- What verse or verses is God using at this time to speak into your life? What is (are) the verse(s) teaching you?

- What actions do you need to take?

Chapter 2
The Calling

For the gifts and the calling of God are irrevocable.
Romans 11:29

While I was going through all the Intervention Radiological procedures, surgery, and recovery, God was at work in my life. During this time, I spent a lot of time at home, which allowed me to read the Bible and pray. As I look back on that time, it was time God used to capture my attention.

The Call

God Spoke

After my home church went through a conflict several years before this adventure with the kidney tumor diagnosis, I had not enjoyed attending church services. Though I know people will disappoint me from time to time, it still hurt to watch some who called themselves brothers in Christ act more as the world behaves than how scriptures teach believers to behave. As God began to speak to me during this time, I started enjoying attending church services again.

One Sunday morning, while I still had the tube in my body, we attended a church service. Since I could not walk well, we entered the Worship Center through a side door that did not have any steps. Within a few steps of entering, we were able to sit down in one of the pews close to the door.

The Worship Center was a fan-shaped auditorium. We could sit on one side of the auditorium and see practically the whole room. The only area we could not see was the balcony area just above where we were sitting.

During the service, my stamina was low, so I sat through the whole service. Besides, with the tube in me moving around every time I moved, it was uncomfortable to stand. I was not expecting God to speak to me that morning, impressing upon me about the condition of men in our culture in 2007.

As I looked across the auditorium and looked at men's faces, I saw many men who did not seem to be excited to be there. I understood because of my previous years—men who seem to be going through the motions. I began to wonder why. I even wondered if this is what I looked like when I attended the worship service in the previous years before all this started.

While I continued to look at these faces, I began to sense many of these men were in the service just because. But just because why? Then it hit me. Many of these men were there for the same reason I was in church for many years. I was raised to be in church on Sunday mornings; even when I was disappointed with the people and leadership, I knew I should be in church. Plus, I had a family, and I need to be an example.

Now don't get me wrong. I was a believer, and I loved the Lord, but for some reason, church services did not excite me during those dark days. But it was ingrained in me from an early age; this is where I was supposed to be on Sunday mornings. We were always in church.

My parents would only accept your absence from church if you were sick or traveling. Otherwise, you will be in the service. So for me, it became a habit. Even after I came to Christ in my senior year in high school, the following Sunday was just another Sunday for me to be in church. For many of those men I was observing, they were there just because they were raised to be in church every Sunday.

Then others had other just because reason:
- Just because my wife wants me here.
- Just because it makes good business sense.
- Just because politically, it looks good.
- Just because I want to be a good example for my children.

The Call

There was nothing wrong with any of these reasons. But were they there because of their love for God or themselves? I sensed many were there for all the wrong reasons.

As I continued to observe these men, a scripture passage came to remembrance, Matthew 7:21-23, one I had read many times, but one I had not fully appreciated what Jesus was saying. However, once I thought about these men and that many were at church just because, it became very real to me. Listen to what Jesus was saying as you read these verses.

"Not everyone who says to me, 'Lord, Lord,' will enter the kingdom of heaven, but the one who does the will of my Father who is in heaven. On that day many will say to me, 'Lord, Lord, did we not prophesy in your name, and cast out demons in your name, and do many mighty works in your name?' And then will I declare to them, 'I never knew you; depart from me, you workers of lawlessness.'"

Matthew 7:21-23

WOW! Did you hear it? Do you realize who Jesus was referring to? Do you understand what Jesus was saying? He was not speaking to those who had nothing to do with Jesus. He was not speaking to those who did not attend church and were not active in the church. These verses are speaking to the people who are involved in the church. Those who are participating in many of the activities of the church. Those who rarely miss a church service.

A Work To Do

I began to realize that though there is much work to be done outside the walls of the church, there is much work to be done within the walls of the church. Many of these men do not have an intentional relationship with Jesus. They may know a lot about Jesus, but they do not know Him, and Jesus does not know them. My heart began to break. I discuss the meaning of this scripture and how it affected me more in Chapter 3.

Several weeks later, as I was recovering and becoming more active, I had an invitation that would continue to change my world further. After a church service one Sunday morning, I was standing in the front of the auditorium speaking with some friends when Mr. Tommy came up to ask me a question.

A Life-Changing Invitation

I have known Mr. Tommy since my early twenties. I met him about the time Joanne and I started dating, which would have been about thirty years earlier. He always gave my family special attention and especially my son, Matt. In fact, Mr. Tommy gave Matt his first job working at his lawn care business. Mr. Tommy is very special to my family, and I always valued him and his wisdom. So if he wants to talk with me, he would have my undivided attention.

Mr. Tommy asked if I would consider joining him with a group of men on Saturday mornings to attend a Bible Study. He

The Call

explained the group meets at a local restaurant early at 6:00 am in the restaurant's private dining room.

I was honored he would ask, and when he continued to explain that Dr. Bill Bennett, Sr. (no, not the political analyst) was leading the group, I was even more interested.

Dr. Bennett, Sr., grew up in the Brunswick County, NC, area, becoming a pastor. One of his pastorates was at the 8,000 member First Baptist Church in Fort Smith, Arkansas, for over twenty years.

I first met Dr. Bennett when I was seventeen years old while he was pastoring in Fort Smith. Calvary Baptist Church in my hometown of Wilmington, NC, invited Dr. Bennett to preach revival each year for several years. I was impressed with his preaching, and he could quote scripture without reading from the Bible. When I first heard him speak, I was amazed at the number of scripture passages he would quote without turning in the Bible to read.

One evening I decided to count the number of passages he would quote in one message, and I stopped counting after one hundred. I contributed it to one who had an eidetic memory. I would later learn it was from years of discipline in scripture memorization.

When Dr. Bennett returned to Wilmington after retiring from the pastorate, he founded the ministry Mentoring Men for the Master. It was a discipling ministry where he poured into the life of other men from his life experiences, his study of the Bible, and where he would encourage scripture memorization.

A verse that he often quoted has become my life verse, 1 Thessalonians 2:8. I would encourage you to memorize this verse. I will reference this verse often throughout this book. The verse states,

"Being affectionately desirous of you, we were ready to share with you not only the gospel of God but also our own selves, because you had become very dear to us."

After Mr. Tommy explained who was leading, I told him I would be there the following Saturday. After attending my first session with Dr. Bennett, I was hooked.

Attending Mentoring Men for the Master

Approximately 40 men attended every week. Dr. Bennett would go around the room asking men how their week was. Then he would pop that dreaded question. "What scripture verse did you memorize this week?" If you told him one, the following statement would be, "Say it for me." So you had better know it or know it enough that Dr. Bennett knew you had been working on it. If you did not work on memorizing one scripture verse during the week, he would politely and lovingly encourage you. In other words, he would give you a spiritual spanking.

He would always have us say a couple of phrases each week as we started our session. One was called the Victory Pledge.

I am too anointed to be disappointed,
I am too blessed to be depressed,

The Call

I am too chosen to be frozen,
I am too elected to be rejected,
I am too inspired to be tired,
I have more to shout about than to pout about,
And I have more to sing about
Then complain about. [1]

The other was called Pledge to my Bible.

This is my Bible.
It is God's inerrant Word.
It is my most valuable earthly possession.
I will, therefore, make it a lamp unto my feet and a light unto my path, and I will hide its words in my heart that I might not sin against God.
The Bible is God talking to me personally.
I will, therefore, listen to it carefully and obey it fully.
And I will endeavor to internalize it in my life by doing four things.
I will Know it in my head by diligent study;
I will Stow it in my heart by memorization and meditation;
I will Show it in my life by obeying its teachings; and
I will Sow it in my world by witnessing.
Hereafter I will never be the same, never, never, never!
In the name of Jesus, for His honor and glory, both now and forever more.
Amen. [2]

Dr. Bennett would then share a message that pertained to a man striving to live in a fallen world to help him walk as a biblical man helping us have a biblical worldview.

For the next three years, I attended faithfully. I will have to say that I learned more and grew more in my spiritual walk with God during those years than I had all the years I had been in church before, over 50 years.

Because of attending the sessions conducted by Dr. Bennett, I started reading the Bible more, memorizing the scriptures, and praying. I redeveloped a personal devotional time that had been lacking for many years. Though I had a devotional time throughout my life, I never really took it seriously until now. I even started listening to the Bible through audio recordings when I could not read, such as driving or even mowing the many acres I had to mow each week. I had even started journaling about what I had read.

Understanding the Call

After my surgery, one of the doctors Joanne worked with offered us her beach house on North Topsail Beach, NC, to spend a week relaxing. She knew what we had been through the last several months, and she wanted to help us get out of the rat race for a while. We took her up on the offer and spent a week in May 2007 at the beach house.

Right before the week at the beach house, I had started reading books on men's ministry. I continued to read those books

The Call

while at the beach. One of the books that spoke to my heart was *Effective Men's Ministry: The Indispensable Toolkit for Your Church*, compiled by members of the National Coalition of Men's Ministry (now known as the National Coalition of Ministering to Men) published in 2001. The other was a book that had just been published the year before in 2006, *No Man Left Behind* by Pat Morley, David Delk, and Brett Clemmer of Man in the Mirror.

Reading these books, my time with Mentoring Men for the Master, and my personal study and prayer time, I understood the need for a church to have a vibrant ministry to men. The hunger in my belly was growing stronger each day. But what was I supposed to do? I did not have any training in ministering to men. I had not even finished college. I started to get my degree later in life, but it would be another two years in 2009 before obtaining my Business Administration degree.

But I kept pressing forward. While at the beach house, I started developing a slide presentation taking information from these books and research I was doing on the web. I did not have a clue what I was doing. I felt as if I was just putting words on a paper.

> *I knew God was getting my attention, and he had more for me to do. But what was it?*

I contacted the Associate Pastor at my church and shared my desire to work with men. He and I met, and I shared the slides with him. We talked and decided to make an appointment with the Senior Pastor to discuss becoming the men's leader of the church. Whoa, dude. Men's Leader. Is that what I am signing up for? Not sure what God had in mind.

When we met with the Sr. Pastor, he was pleased to have someone step up because he had been doing all the work up to this point. Of course, he did not have the time required to develop a vibrant ministry to men because, as the Pastor, he had so much on his plate already. He was eager for me to take the reins as long as I kept him in the loop.

So, I began a new adventure.

God Continued to Speak

During the summer of 2007, I was mowing our many acres one day on the Zero Turn Radius (ZTR) mower. I always wear a headset while mowing for two reasons; it protects my ear from the ZTR noise, and I can listen to a media source to pass the time. This time I was listening to Paul Washer, a Protestant evangelist. I cannot tell you what he was speaking on, but he mentioned a scripture, and it stopped me in my tracks. I sat on the mower, replaying the section where he said the scripture probably three or four times. The scripture pierced into my very soul.

Up to this time, I had no clue what was in store for me as I was still working through my cancer diagnosis, surgery, and recovery. But this scripture confirmed to me that God was not through with me. It was then I knew God was getting my attention, and he had more for me to do. But what was it? Oh, the scripture? It was Psalms 71:18. It still is a meaningful scripture

The Call

to me. "Even when I am old and gray, O God, do not forsake me, Until I declare Your strength to this generation, Your power to all who are to come." (NASB)

Another time, during my hour commute to the office one morning after returning to work, I was listening to K-Love, a national Christian radio station, when they played a song that spoke to me. It was a song that had been around for a while; I knew it and enjoyed the song. I had listened to it on the radio before and heard it sung in church. But for some reason, this time, it was like God was speaking the words directly to me. I was brought to tears as I listened to the words. I even remember where I was on the commute. I was driving south on US17 out of Wilmington, NC, and was getting ready to turn on to South NC87 in Winnabow, NC. It was about 5:30 in the morning.

The song was *You Raise Me Up*, sung by the group Selah. The words helped me realize God was going to see me through this. Let these partial lyrics speak to you if you are going through difficult times in your life now. Look up the entire song, and you will be blessed.

> When I am down and oh, my soul so weary
> When troubles come and my heart burdened be
> Then I am still and wait here in the silence
> Until You come and sit awhile with me
>
> You raise me up so I can stand on mountains
> You raise me up to walk on stormy seas
> I am strong when I am on Your shoulders

You raise me up to more than I can be. [3]

It was like God was speaking directly in my life through the chorus, saying that He has raised me up to stand on mountains, He has raised me up to walk on the stormy seas, that I am strong when He puts me on His shoulders, and He will raise me up to be more than I can be. I can remember this as if it were yesterday.

A Men's Ministry Leader

Besides reading those two books I mentioned earlier and a few others, I still had no clue what to do or how to do it. I still had to rely on the pastors for their wisdom and encouragement.

At my church, we called our men's ministry Ironman. How original. Based on Proverbs 27:17, "Iron sharpens iron, and one man sharpens another." Pretty original, wasn't it? It did not take long for me to discover that most men's groups called themselves Ironmen or some semblance.

I started making connections with other leaders of men's ministries from around the area. I discovered they were like me regarding the knowledge of how to have an effective ministry to men. All the pastors had ideas, but most ideas were gleaned from the material they had read and not from experience.

One of the books I read early on, *No Man Left Behind*, was written by three men who were leaders of Man in the Mirror, an organization dedicated to training and equipping men to be leaders in their churches and develop leadership teams to create sustainable ministries.

Man in the Mirror at the time had field representatives throughout the United States. I contacted them and applied to be a field representative. It was an interesting process as they vetted you to determine if you would be a good candidate for the position. They required a letter from your wife to see how she felt about you working in this ministry area and determining what she thought of you as a husband. I sweated bullets on this one as Joanne did not like writing letters like this anyway. They required your pastor to write a letter of recommendation, plus I was interviewed by a Man in the Mirror staff member. Finally, you had to attend a No Man Left Behind Training weekend. I attended one held in Knoxville, TN, where Brett Clemmer would be conducting the training. Brett at the time was Vice-President of Man in the Mirror.

> ...most men in our churches did not know how to lead men.

At this training, I realized most men in our churches did not know how to lead men. Even many of the pastors of churches did not know how to organize and lead men. Most of the men's ministry programs ("program" is not a word I like to associate with men's ministry) were activity-based and generally had just one leader who led the ministry.

Over time I discovered two things; first, an activity-based men's ministry does not grow spiritually-minded men with a biblical worldview. The second item is if a single man leads a church men's ministry, then when that leader quits or leaves the church, the men's ministry dies. In some smaller churches, the pastor is the men's ministry leader. He already has a lot on his plate, so his time of involvement in the men's ministry is limited. Plus, if he leaves to accept a position at another church or organization, the men's ministry dies.

The realization of a leadership team's importance to oversee the men's ministry of a respective church is paramount. Though it does need to incorporate some activities, the men's ministry must be built as a discipleship-based ministry. Anything short of this will be a moral failure.

A Men's Ministry Mentor

Through Man in the Mirror, I met a men's pastor, Jeff Kisiah, who became my mentor for several years. He is the one who helped me understand the importance of one man pouring into another and multiplying that into other men. At the time, he was the Men's Pastor at Harvest Community Church in Concord, NC. He later became the National Field Director for Man in the Mirror, to whom all of us working in the field reported.

He became a good friend and mentor until the Lord called him home on May 3, 2019. Through his ministry and encouragement, he helped me understand God's calling on my life as a ministry to men to help leaders and churches reach their men. Much of what you will read in the rest of the book will be teachings and insights he instilled in me and many others he has mentored.

The Call

Let me encourage you in closing this chapter; if you are a men's ministry leader in your church, find a mentor to help you become more effective in your ministering to men.

Questions to reflect on for your next step.

- What is the one thing that you are passionate about? What burdens you?

- Have you ever considered what you are passionate about or burdened with as what God is calling you to do? Explain.

- Are you doing what you believe God has called you to do? Explain.

- What actions do you need to take?

The Call

Chapter 3
Just Because

"Not everyone who says to me, 'Lord, Lord,' will enter the kingdom of heaven, but the one who does the will of my Father who is in heaven.

Matthew 7:21

In the previous chapter, I mentioned Matthew 7:21-23. The scripture started me thinking about the work that needs to be done within our churches' walls—speaking into the lives of the number of men who attend church each week, going through the motions and not growing spiritually, and those not developing a biblical worldview.

In this chapter, I want to unpack those verses to understand what Jesus was telling us. I have read Matthew's Gospel numerous times in my life, especially the Sermon on the Mount, where we find the text. But never until that fateful Sunday morning, when I was looking at the men's faces, did I understand all too clearly what Jesus was saying—and frankly, it scared me. These words were one of the final words of the warning that He gave to the people listening to Him on that mount. Unfortunately, just like many men in our churches today, the people listening to Jesus on that mount probably did not understand the implications of what Jesus was saying.

At the conclusion of Matthew's account of the Sermon on the Mount, Matthew penned these words in Matthew 7:28 to help us understand the people's reaction to what they had just witnessed. "And when Jesus finished these sayings, the crowds were astonished at his teaching."

They were astonished at all that Jesus said as they saw Him as "teaching them as one who had authority" (Mat. 7:29).

A Men's Ministry Leader Should Understand This Text

These words in Matthew 7:21-23 should resonate with every men's leader. It should help him recognize that not every man sitting in the pews of their church, who is active in the church's work, will make it to glory.

A Journey Into Men's Ministry

When I was thirteen years old, my Pastor visited me and told me it was time for me to join the church. He stated that all my peers had joined the church, and I was one of the few who had not in my age group. However, he never shared a word of the gospel message or that I needed to surrender my life to Christ.

His approach could have resulted in me being one of those who would have gone through my life saying "Lord, Lord," but in the end would have heard Jesus say, "Depart from me you son of lawlessness, I never knew you." That pastor never spoke to me about the saving grace of Christ and never even mentioned the gospel message. His only concern was for me to "walk the aisle" and join the church.

Speaking with many over the years, I discovered some were encouraged to join a church but never heard the gospel message. Church leaders who never repented of this process of just adding members to their church rolls will have to answer for influencing people who became inoculated against the gospel message because they had joined the church. How many have you heard make the statement "because they are a member of a church" when asked how they know they are a Christian? Jesus knew this was going to happen, and He warned the people 2,000 years ago.

Listen to these words carefully. Read them slowly. Let them sink in so you can meditate on them. After reading, we will unpack these words and look at what it means to many people.

Matthew 7:21-23, Matthew recorded these words of Jesus.

The Call

"Not everyone who says to me, 'Lord, Lord,' will enter the kingdom of heaven, but the one who does the will of my Father who is in heaven. On that day many will say to me, 'Lord, Lord, did we not prophesy in your name, and cast out demons in your name, and do many mighty works in your name?' And then will I declare to them, 'I never knew you; depart from me, you workers of lawlessness.'"

Lord, Lord

Now let us begin to unpack this text, starting with verse 21. "Not everyone who says to me, 'Lord, Lord,' will enter the kingdom of heaven, but the one who does the will of my Father who is in heaven."

A Gallop Poll in 2016-2018 reported 52% of the people in the United States in 2016-2018, on average, are members of a church. [4] We have to ask how many of those who are members of a church are true believers. According to Barna Research, roughly 35% of the US population claim to be born-again Christians. These individuals have made a personal commitment to Jesus Christ that is still important in their life today and believe that, when they die, they will go to heaven because they have confessed their sins and accepted Jesus Christ as their savior. [5]

Imagine you are sitting in your church during a service and looking around at all the people attending. Your church may have 20, 30, or maybe 100 people in attendance. Maybe your church has greater than a hundred, maybe 500 or more. Perhaps your church is one of those that might have 1,000 or more in attendance. But whatever the number, we know all are not followers of Christ. According to the Barna Research mentioned earlier, maybe 35% of the people attending are true believers. In some churches, the number may be higher, and some it will be lower. There will be some in attendance who have rejected God's call to be one of His. But is this verse speaking about those individuals? I do not believe so.

Now look around at all the men in attendance, no matter the size of your church. What do you see? Who is there? Men of all ages. Men of various socio-economic status. Men who are single and married. Men who have children and some who do not. The point is there are men with varying positions in life attending church. Many of those men are eager to worship God and participate in many Christian life activities.

Some of these men—possibly many—are false confessors of the faith in Christ. However, their inward nature has not changed; they merely wear the outward guise of a believer. They refer to Christ as Lord and even do deeds as a believer, as we will see as we continue to unpack the text, but they are not saved.

How do we detect these false believers? Matthew 7:16 tells us how. "You will recognize them by their fruits." By their fruit.

What fruit is Christ looking for from these that cried 'Lord, Lord?' We can begin with the attitude one would have described at the beginning of the Sermon on the Mount in Matthew 5. Verses three through eleven give an account of how believers should behave. We refer to them as the Beatitudes.

Galatians 5:22-23 explains the fruit of the Spirit for true believers. These are the characteristics of a true believer. "But the fruit of the Spirit is love, joy, peace, patience, kindness, goodness, faithfulness, gentleness, self-control."

God also looks for the fruit of our lips that acknowledges His name, giving testimony and praise (Heb. 13:15). Next, he looks for holy living (Rom. 6:22). Next, he looks for individuals doing good works (Col. 1:10). Finally, God is looking for those who seek to win lost souls to Christ (Rom. 1:13). [6]

By having these attitudes and characteristics in one's life, you will be doing the will of the Father who is in Heaven. John 14:15 reminds us that Jesus stated, "If you love me, you will keep my commandments." These are the people God is looking for who say "Lord, Lord." If the Lord does not find these qualities, His Word says they will not enter the kingdom of Heaven.

They Begin to Justify Themselves

Verse 22 of Matthew 7 states, "On that day many will say to me, 'Lord, Lord, did we not prophesy in your name, and cast out demons in your name, and do many mighty works in your name?'"

Now the people are beginning to rationalize with Jesus. "Look what we did!" They will exclaim, "Look at all the work we did in your name. We did it for you!"

Many active in the church may be involved in various church and community works and act like saved believers but do not have a relationship with Jesus. The works they are doing are to bring recognition to themselves. The fruits we discussed earlier do not bear out in their daily lives.

Note that these people will be surprised when they stand before God at the Judgment. The Scriptures teach us Satan will blind the mind and deceive people into thinking they are true believers (2 Cor. 4:3-4). Satan is the god of this age and has blinded unbelievers' minds, even many who believe they are true believers.

Often, we get upset when people act or say things that are totally against scripture, even trying to keep scripture out of society. We need to remember that it is not their reasoning that makes them go against the Bible; it is the fact that Satan has blinded them, and they cannot see the truth. We need to show compassion to these people and not feel threatened or show anger.

Just like Paul, who had scales on his eyes after encountering Jesus on the road to Damascus, these people have scales on their minds and hearts that only the Holy Spirit can remove. Instead of getting frustrated, upset, or even angry with those against the Bible, we need to be praying the Holy Spirit will pierce their hearts so they can see the light of the gospel of Christ, who is the image of God (2 Cor. 11:14-15).

We can look to Jesus' disciples and see this played out. Remember Judas Iscariot? He was one of the twelve Jesus picked to be part of His inner circle. He taught and shared some of his most treasured thoughts, preparing them for His ultimate death and resurrection though they did not realize what He was teaching until after His resurrection.

Judas did what all the rest of the disciples did. In fact, Judas was among the twelve known as Jesus' apostles (Mark 3:14). In Matthew 10, Jesus sent the apostles out to the people of Israel to preach that the Kingdom of Heaven is near. Judas would have been part of this group. They were given specific instructions to heal the sick, raise the dead, cure those with leprosy, and cast out demons (vs. 6-8).

In Mark 6:30, the apostles returned from being sent out, excited while they were telling Jesus all they had done and taught. Judas Iscariot was no doubt among them, most likely showing the same tremendous excitement.

But Judas, even with all of his excitement of doing the work of Christ, never surrendered to God. Instead, he sought his own direction. He took his own course of action, rejecting God's plan. He went to the religious leaders to devise a plan that some biblical scholars believe was to get Jesus to establish His kingdom on earth by forcing him to reveal Himself as the Son of God and establish His kingdom here on earth. Then when Judas realized his mistake, he became so remorseful for what he had done in his betrayal of Jesus, he committed suicide (Matt. 27:5).

Read what Dr. Ray Pritchard says about Judas in his article What Happened to Judas?

"In terms of experience, whatever you can say about James, Peter and John, you can say also about Judas. Everywhere they went, he also went. He was right there, always by the side of Jesus. He heard it all, saw it all, experienced it all. However you explain his defection, you cannot say he was less experienced than the other apostles.

If anything, he was one of the leaders. After all, the other apostles chose him to handle the money. You don't pick a man whose loyalty you suspect to handle your money. That's crazy. You pick your best man, your most trustworthy man, the one man you know you can count on. That's why they picked Judas.

The most interesting part of this story is that the other apostles apparently saw only the positive side of Judas. It wasn't until they looked back after the fact that they could see the negatives. Before his betrayal of Jesus, he looked as good as any of the rest, and in fact he probably looked better than most. In that light, let us note it for the record one more time: No one suspected Judas. No one." [7]

Judas was like those in our churches today who are fellowshipping with believers, doing the work of the church, yet have never surrendered to God.

We, of course, do not know who has truly surrendered to God. Only God knows the true intent of the heart of the man. But I cannot help but think about the witness and example of many I have encountered in my life who talked the talk but failed miserably to walk the walk as a daily example. I do not mean men who fell into temptation and required help in getting back up, but those who deliberately walked in the ways of the world.

When I first went to work for Carolina Power and Light at age nineteen, I came across one of the Sunday School teachers I had in Junior High who was also an employee. As a young Christian, my thoughts were great: I have one of my earliest mentors

The Call

to help guide me through life in the real world. God had provided one of my earliest mentors for me to work alongside to continue to guide me. What I did not realize was that God was getting ready to teach me a lesson.

It did not take long before I heard language from my former Sunday School teacher that I never thought I would hear. I did not hear him talking like this when we were at church or church gatherings and socials. But here he was stringing words together like a drunken sailor (my apologies to the sailors) that could make anyone within earshot blush with embarrassment.

After I got the courage to do so, I remember approaching him, which was many days later, to question him about his language. He was standing at a desk we used to write job reports when I approached him. I said, "Mr. John (not his real name), why do you curse like you do? You told us in Sunday School years ago this is not how we are to talk. Why do you do it?"

He replied without ever looking up from what he was doing, "Do what I say and not what I do," We've heard that old *cliché* often when joking, but this time he was not kidding. He did not want to discuss it, and we never did. But it did bother me to the point I went and talked to my pastor.

It was my first encounter with someone I saw in church every Sunday, served as a Sunday School teacher to young boys, served as a deacon in the church, yet was not living in the manner he was teaching. His attitude and character did not bear the fruit of the spirit.

After Joanne and I were married, we were helping with the youth ministry at the church we were attending. We had a man helping who was in the church services every Sunday. He had one of those license plates on the front of his truck that advertised a local bar and club that he frequented regularly. The man was questioned about it, and he blew it off as no big deal. He just made some statements about liking to have a good time on weekends. Again seemingly not exhibiting the fruit of the spirit.

Or how about when there is a situation in the church that must be confronted. You will discover who is walking in the Spirit by the fruit they exhibit in these times. I remember when I was serving as the Secretary of the Deacon Board of my church. I had to moderate a church business meeting because the Chairman and Vice-Chairman could not be at the meeting. The situation got tense, and individuals were making statements with attitudes that did not honor God. I threatened to suspend the meeting to another time unless everyone calmed down and began to act in a manner that would honor God. I challenged them because those who called themselves believers were not acting in the fruit of the spirit described in Galatians 5 or the character of those whom Christ described at the beginning of Matthew 5 (Beatitudes).

> *You will discover who is walking in the Spirit by the fruit they exhibit.*

Let me make it clear: I do not know the relationship status of any of these individuals with Christ, my Sunday School teacher, the man helping with the youth, or the individuals in the church business meeting. I just know they were not behaving as one should if they have indeed been transformed as the scripture tells us about becoming a new creation (2 Cor. 5:15). Only God knows our hearts, and many in our churches today are living deceptive lives thinking they are children of God but are not.

I Never Knew You

Those who are not doing the will of the father will eventually hear Christ say, "I never knew you, depart from me, you workers of lawlessness" (Matt. 5:23).

These are harsh words, and many in our churches today will be surprised when they hear them. They will try and rationalize with Jesus all the work they had done.

"Jesus, I served as a Sunday School teacher."

"Jesus, I was on the Deacon Board."

"Jesus, I helped the homeless."

"Jesus, I spent time helping the widows and orphans."

Even, "Jesus, I preached the gospel message." Well, even Judas Iscariot did that.

Several years ago, I had a conversation with a man in his 70s who told me about his wife. When he married her, he thought if anyone were going to be in heaven at death, it would be her. She was always ministering in the church in some manner. Ten years into their marriage, she woke him one night as she realized her need for Christ and that she had never surrendered her life to God. He told me that night she gave her life to Christ, and even after being one who was always working in the church, he saw a change in her.

Obedience to His will is the test of true faith in Christ. It is easy to learn a religious vocabulary, even memorize Bible verses and spiritual songs like the man's wife did, and yet not obey God's will. When a person is genuinely born again, he has the Spirit of God living within (Rom. 8:9), and the Spirit enables him to know and do the will of the Father. God's love in his heart (Rom. 5:5) motivates him to obey God and serve others.

Words are not a substitute for obedience, and neither are religious works. Preaching, casting out demons, and performing miracles can be divinely inspired, but they give no assurance of salvation. Once again, look at Judas Iscariot.

Judas Iscariot likely participated in some or all of these activities, yet he was not a true believer. In the last days, Satan will use "lying wonders" to deceive people (2 Thess. 2:7-12).

In Dr. David Jeremiah's book, *Agents of the Apocalypse*, there is a fictional story of a man who was active in the church. His name in the story was Morgan. He did all the things asked of him to help the cause of the local body of believers. Yet when he died, he stood at the judgment seat of Christ and discovered he was heading to the lake of fire to be separated from God for eternity. Here is an excerpt from that story. It helps one visualize what will happen to those who are just going through the motions. It begins with Jesus speaking to Morgan.

"Morgan, as your books have already shown, you did the visible things that brought you praise. Everything you did was for you, not for the love of others. You cannot love Me if you do not love others. You never loved Me, Morgan. Though you wore My name, you were an impostor. You said the right words, but your heart belonged to you." "But what about grace?" Morgan cried. "Can't You give me grace?" "My grace was always available to you. All you had to do was place your trust in Me and make Me the Lord of your life. Had you done that, My grace would have freely covered your sins and failures. But you never surrendered yourself and allowed Me into your heart. Therefore, you never knew Me, and I never knew you." [8]

Where Do You Stand?

Here is the time you need to reflect and determine your relationship with Jesus. As you review your life, you need to decide whether you are doing all the work you do in the church for yourself or the kingdom of God? Where is your heart? Does it belong to Jesus?

Did you join a church to say you are a church member, and because of this, you believe you will spend eternity with God? Are you like the wife of the gentleman I shared earlier who knew how to talk the talk because she grew up in the church but never surrendered her life to Christ? Are you one inoculated against the gospel message because a church leader told you all you had to do was present yourself for church membership?

If you answered any of these questions with a "yes" and can never say you have repented of your sins and surrendered your life to Christ, then do so now, before you go any further in this book.

A Journey Into Men's Ministry

There is a children's song we used to sing that reminds me of how to behave. Though it will not make sure you have a genuine relationship with the Father, it reminds us that the Father is viewing our behavior, and He knows if our heart is tuned to Him. The song was *O Be Careful Little Eyes*. Read the lyrics below and let the Holy Spirit speak to you.

O be careful little eyes what you see
O be careful little eyes what you see
For the Father up above
is looking down in love
So, be careful little eyes what you see
O be careful little ears what you hear
O be careful little ears what you hear
For the Father up above
is looking down in love
So, be careful little ears what you hear
O be careful little tongue what you say
O be careful little tongue what you say
For the Father up above
is looking down in love
So, be careful little tongue what you say
O be careful little hands what you do
O be careful little hands what you do
For the Father up above
is looking down in love
So, be careful little hands what you do
O be careful little feet where you go

The Call

O be careful little feet where you go
For the Father up above
is looking down in love
So, be careful little feet where you go. [9]

I pray you have given your life to Christ, and all the work you are doing in the church is for God and not for yourself. If you are not sure or have never surrendered your life to Christ, I encourage you to go to Appendix 1, The Roman Road, read through the scriptures, and trust in the Lord today.

If you do that, be sure you tell someone in your church what you just did. If you are not involved with a church, you can email me at capefearmen@gmail.com and tell me. I would enjoy hearing about your commitment.

A Journey Into Men's Ministry

Questions to reflect on for your next step.

- Why do you attend church services?

- Have you truly surrendered your life to Christ, or are you just going through the motions? Share your story.

- Have you ever thought about the number of men in your church who are going through the motions? Do you think there may be a concern?

- What actions do you need to take?

The Call

Chapter 4
Leading Your Men

Where there is no guidance, a people falls, but in an abundance of counselors there is safety.
                    Proverbs 11:14

Is your church targeting the men attending? If not, why not? I often hear pastors talk about how they value their men, but rarely do they speak about the lives of men from the pulpit. Their churches rarely plan events centered around men. But they expect the men to attend Sunday School and discipleship group meetings. Some men will attend Sunday School, and a few may become connected with a discipleship group.

The Call

Being one who works in men's ministry and had worked with youth in the early years of my life, I see many similarities. Many wives often describe their husbands as a child in a grown-up body, and in some cases, they are probably not far from the truth. Like with the youth, we plan events and activities to give us opportunities to invest our lives into them and share the gospel message. We do the same with men. Yet instead of going to the beach (unless it is to fish), amusement parks, or lock-ins, you plan fishing trips, golf scrambles, trips to the big game or NASCAR, wild game nights, etc.

We encourage men to attend these events to develop relationships and encourage them to attend Bible studies or discipleship groups, which prods them toward the next step. These events allow men not attending Sunday Schools or home study groups or discipleship groups to hear from men attending, hopefully creating an interest for those who do not attend one of these groups.

Targeting Your Men

The ministries of most churches rarely, if ever, have events that center around men. I have even heard of a church that stated we don't need a formalized ministry to men. But interestingly, whether they have a formalized ministry to men or not, they have one—they just don't realize it. The church will either tell the men they are valuable and care about them or tell them they are not valuable.

Some churches will intentionally target the men because they know that as the man goes, so goes the family, and so goes the church body. One such church is Mecklenburg Community Church in Charlotte, NC, whose senior pastor, Dr. James Emery White, lists targeting men as one of their eight strategic decisions. He states that these eight decisions have proven to be tactical in serving their mission as a church.

In their description of targeting men in their eight strategic decisions, the church states;

"At Meck, we unashamedly target men in our outreach, in our messages, in our... well, almost everything. We have become convinced through years of experience that if you get the man, you get everyone else within his orbit—specifically, his wife and his children.

What does it mean to target men? It means you think about male sensibilities in terms of music and message, vocabulary, and style. One of the most frequent things we hear from women is: "My husband loves this church. I could never get him to church before. But now he comes here even when I don't!" And she will go where he wants to go. Get him, you get her. Get him and her, you get the family. It's as simple as that." [10]

It appears that Dr. White and The Meck get it. If you want to reach the complete family, you need to target the men intentionally. Churches historically have ministries that speak to children, youth, ladies, even families as a whole. Still, they rarely have ministries that speak directly into the hearts and minds of the individual men.

During one of the meeting times with my mentor Jeff Kisiah, he shared about a visit to a church where he spoke to the men. As he was touring the church campus, he came across a table in the church's vestibule. He found small wire baskets with brochures that provided information about key ministries of the church on the table. The brochures in the individual baskets were on the Women's Ministry, the Youth Ministry, and the Children's Ministry. What was missing was one for the men's ministry. One would have to ask themselves visiting the church, does this church genuinely value the men, and are they serious about ministering to men? Are they targeting their men?

I have discovered another interesting fact from reviewing churches' websites. Very few websites have anything on the site targeting men. Most will have information on the children and youth ministries, and occasionally, you will find information regarding the women's ministries. Information on the men's ministry will be missing.

Churches who are targeting their men will take every opportunity to reach and connect with them. I encourage you to use every means possible to show the men they are important to the church's life.

Recently, I was invited to attend a men's event sponsored by a church. During the event, I discovered they were planning a Bible study for their men. I was applauding them for creating another entry point for their men. Then I found, they waited to announce the study five days before they were to start. Even more interesting, the Bible study announcement was made only to the men who attended the event—less than a hundred from a church of over 2,500. Does this sound like a church that is targeting its men?

I encourage you to examine what you are doing to reach the men connected with your church, especially those on the fringes. Such as the man in church regularly but not involved in any discipling relationship or even attending men's events. What are you doing to reach these men? Because most churches don't intentionally target men, I wonder if that contributes to most men thinking the church is just for women and children. That is something to think about.

Identify a Men's Pastor

I was recently on a conference call with a number of our National Coalition of Ministering to Men members when one of them made this statement, "Churches who are serious about men have a man at a staff level position to serve as the Men's Pastor." He clarified his statement to help understand he was not necessarily talking about having someone in a paid position; it could be a layperson. The point is to have someone listed as a staff member known as the men's pastor or leader who is called to minister to men. Whenever people look at the church's website or review a document that lists the church staff, men, and women visiting the church will see a Men's Pastor identified. Visitors will understand the church is serious about the men.

Developing Relationships

This book discusses being intentional in developing relationships with men to help them move into discipling groups. We also discuss the concept of creating entry points and getting to know the men connected with your church. If the church's men and the leadership team display these concepts, you will find the ministry to the men beginning to take on a new life.

Many men who are active in the church generally desire to reach out and help individuals in need. Many of the men in our churches are involved in helping with maintenance activities around the church. They may be helping with a recovery effort after a devastating storm has come through an area. They might be involved in building ramps to make homes more accessible to the disabled. The men may even go on various types of mission trips. But does that mean the men are equipped to do ministry? I will submit to you—not necessarily.

In my travels, I have seen men working hard to deal with an individual's specific needs. They may have been trained to do the task assigned, and they do an exceptional job. But there is another aspect that equips men to minister to the spiritual needs of the individual.

When men are being established in spiritual maturity, they will begin to acquire the tools to speak into people's lives. Generally, these men will be the first to volunteer for ministering opportunities.

Meeting the Spiritual Needs

Often, men trained in specific tasks have not been prepared to share the gospel, pray with and for someone, or respond to people when they ask "Why?" when going through difficult times. They like helping the physical needs but often lack the skills to deal with the spiritual needs.

When on a ministry opportunity, encourage team members to develop a relationship with the recipient of the ministry. Not everyone on the team will be able to do this; but, someone in the group may be able to relate personally with the individual. Take the time to get to know them and, at some point, talk with them about spiritual matters. I have noticed men who have been in discipling relationships are more likely to develop those relationships with the individual. It is essential to help move our men into discipling relationships to develop the spiritual maturity to speak into others' lives. As a men's leader, that should be your number one goal.

As men grow spiritually in their walk with God, they will develop the confidence to speak in addition to providing physical ministry. There is a direct correlation between establishing men in spiritual maturity and equipping men to the ministry.

Equipping men to minister is two-fold: (1) teach them how to perform tasks that meet the individual's needs and (2) speak to the individual about spiritual matters. This is accomplished by getting men involved in training opportunities to learn the tasks and discipling relationships to speak into lives.

Evaluating the Men's Ministry

As you evaluate your church's ministry to men, check to be sure you are not only training them to perform specific tasks exceptionally well, but the ministry is also discipling the men so they can speak to others with confidence.

One of the keys to helping men become the men they were created to be is helping them understand their need for Christ. Since we are made in the image of God (Gen. 1:26), we need to have our spiritual life right to become the man God expects us to be. Therefore, share the gospel message often.

When we plan events, we need to always keep in mind the opportunities to tell the gospel message. How that message is conveyed can vary depending on the venue and event. For instance, in a gathering over a meal, the gospel message could be told through someone's testimony recognizing their need for Christ and surrendering. A participatory event such as golf, fishing, or other activity could provide material such as a gospel tract supplied in a gift bag or even through a devotional before the event.

This cornerstone should be considered every time an event is planned. NEVER assume every man who attends a church event has a personal relationship with Christ. Many will appear to have a relationship, but Jesus may one day look at them and say, "I never knew you" (Matt. 7:23).

Remember the story I spoke of in the previous chapter about the man's wife? He thought if anyone were going to heaven, it would be her only to discover she had never surrendered her life to Christ? You have many men sitting in your church in this condition.

At events, never assume the men attending have accepted Christ as their savior because they are always in church and participate in ministries. Remember Judas; all the disciples thought he was one of them because he participated in all their activities—there may be one in your midst who, though may be not a betrayer like Judas, may not be like you in Christ.

Your leadership team should always plan a method to present the gospel message with the men you connect with. Your leadership team is central to targeting your men and maintaining an effective and vibrant ministry to men. This group of men should constantly be thinking of ways to connect with the men. But so often, I find the leadership team is one man, and generally, it is someone who the church looked for to fill out their positions each year.

The Call

Men's Ministry Leadership

Here's the problem with having a one-man men's ministry leadership. What happens when that one man's job transfers him to another city? What happens when he gets burnt out from the responsibility? What happens if the Lord decides to call him home? In the majority of the cases, if he had anything going on, it ends right there. There is no one to take over and keep the ministry going. This is why it is important—essential—that churches have a men's ministry leadership team. One man cannot maintain the ministry by himself. Even if the church has a Men's Pastor on staff, they need a leadership team.

In the book *No Man Left Behind*, the authors discuss the importance of having three strands of leadership: an enthusiastic pastor, a passionate leader, and a committed leadership team. [11]

The pastor is not the leader of the men's ministry but is a strong supporter. He speaks to the men regularly. He helps get the information out to the men from the platform, and he is a sounding board for the leadership team. As men's leaders, we have to remember he is the pastor of the whole church. He has enough on his plate without us adding to it by expecting him to plan and oversee men's activities.

A passionate leader is someone who feels called to this position. Never . . . Let me repeat this. Never assign someone in your church to be the men's ministry leader because the nominating committee has to fill a position. This is the quickest way for the ministry to men to fail. It is better not to fill the position than to put someone there who does not have the desire and has only agreed because he does not want to let the church down—or feels pressure. This man needs to have a calling to minister to men. Like a pastor is called to preach, a men's ministry leader is called to minister to men, and no matter what he does, he cannot shake the feeling of the call. I believe God has placed a man in every church for this calling. We need to pray and seek him out—God will reveal it to the man if he listens. Pray that the man will listen to God.

The third part of the leadership group is the team of men working alongside the leader. These are men who have a passion in particular areas. If possible, your team should be men representing the generations of the church's men and men with different interests. As we will discuss in the following chapters, you have men in your church with different interests. The desire is to have a leadership team that can tap into each of those interests. Find men who not only have a passion for reaching men but who are passionate about something.

For instance, maybe you have an avid fisherman, a hunter, or one who likes to dive into God's Word through Bible study. Perhaps you have a man who likes to golf, wants to plan retreats, attend conferences, or do mission projects. Each of these men is a potential member of your leadership team. Have them pray about coming on board so you can combine your energy toward reaching the men of your church. Each of these men would be the lead for developing an outing or activity in their passionate area. The rest of the team supports that leader in any way they can. I would caution you not to plan an activity until you have a passionate team member passionate about the activity.

A scripture you will hear me quote often is Ecclesiastes 4:9, "Two are better than one because they have a good return for their labor" (NASB). Here are a couple more scriptures that help us understand the importance of having a leadership team. Proverbs 11:14, "Where there is no guidance, a people falls, but in an abundance of counselors there is safety," and Proverbs 24:6, "By wise guidance you can wage your war, and in abundance of counselors there is victory."

The Bible coaches us as men's leaders the importance of having a team of counselors walking beside us as we develop an effective and vibrant ministry to men.

Decorate for Men

Finally, in this chapter, let's talk about church décor. Now you may be saying, "What does church décor have to do with ministering to men?" Well, frankly, a lot. When men are in surroundings that have a masculine feel, they are more comfortable. They feel the church considers the men important.

Let's face it; most churches are decorated with a feminine touch. Lovely pastel colors, flowers are sitting on tables, doilies on the tables the flowers set on. Not very inviting for a man. Even in the men's bathrooms, there is a feminine touch. We have to make the churches more inviting for the man. There is nothing in most traditional churches that appeals to a man that would make him feel welcome. Why cannot churches have more of a masculine feel?

Let me give you some examples.

Several years ago, I was teaching a men's class. When I was shown the room where I would be teaching, I gave a little one of those fist bumps of pulling the arm back, saying, "Yeh!" The room had pictures of classic cars and motorcycles on the walls—a picture of an old soda shop. There was an old bench seat from a 1957 Chevrolet Belair in the corner of the room. A few high tables and chairs to match, and in a few places in the room were arcade games. Yes, the room was generally used to minister to the youth, but it was a great place to meet with the men. (Remember the correlation between youth and men I mentioned earlier.) I had thirty men attending the meetings for the next six months, and it evolved into a time of fellowship with meals before we started the study each week.

Some time ago, someone sent me some pictures of a men's bathroom in their church they had redecorated. The photos showed they had hung various tools men may use. There were trowels, handsaw, bit-and-brace, a crosscut saw, and hacksaw hanging on the walls—a 4-foot level hanging vertically between the mirrors. On the table in the room was a couple of toolboxes— Manly sayings in nice wooden frames hanging over the urinals and elsewhere in the room. The baby-changing station located in the room was decorated in camouflage, and get this; the door handle on the door exiting the bathroom was a claw hammer that had been welded and bolted to a corrugated plate and bolted to the door.

If the ladies can decorate their bathrooms in lovely frilly items, why cannot the men decorate theirs with masculine manly items?

I spoke to a men's group one time that was meeting in a garage that was turned into the church's man cave for the men to meet. I currently attend a men's Bible study meeting in an old skating rink that now has the masculine feel as it has been partially demolished on the inside.

Another time I was in Spartanburg, SC, attending a Men's Ministry Leadership training at a local church. We started talking about making the churches feel more manly, and one of the church members said during a break, "Com'on, I want to show you something." So we all started following him into another building. The building had high ceilings and in the back, there was a caged basketball court. As we arrived at the basketball court, he pointed up. There before us was a fully restored P-31 World War II training aircraft hanging in the ceiling. What man would not be impressed with that?

I know every church cannot hang an aircraft from the ceiling, but I think you are getting the picture. Every church can change the décor in the men's restroom to be masculine and create a room as a man-cave where men meet for studies.

Some churches are painting the walls in the worship centers a darker color instead of the bright white. More churches incorporate bands and sing masculine songs periodically, and if they utilize videos during the services, they occasionally speak to the man. The dress code has even changed. Men see they do not have to wear a coat and tie to church anymore, and they can dress down. Now let me say I still believe men need to be respectful in their dress, but what if a man comes in wearing shorts. I am interested in reaching the man and having that man become the man God wants him to be as a husband, dad, employer, employee, or friend. I don't care if he does it in a business suit or shorts.

The Call

Men's Ministry is in the Business of Reaching Men

The idea is that we are in the business with God to reach men. We need men to feel welcome when they arrive at church. When men see someone on the church staff identified as a men's pastor, it lets the man and, if married, his wife know this church must be serious about ministering to men. When the church décor is not entirely feminine but has some masculine appeal, it helps the men feel welcome. When masculine songs are sung and manly videos are shown, it will minister to the male psyche, encouraging them to be engaging. Men need this. Why?

Because men are in a battle. We are in The Battle for Men's Souls. Michael Thompson, in his book *The Heart of a Warrior*, makes this statement, "My work with men these past twenty years has convinced me that men are either entering a battle, they are in a battle, or they are emerging from one." [12] Again, this should encourage us to develop an effective and vibrant ministry to men with a dedicated and passionate leadership team that will guide and direct them through their daily battles—giving them a solid foundation on which to stand.

Ministering to men is hard work. It is one of the hardest, if not the hardest, ministries a church will do. Notice I did not say undertake because ministering to men for a church is a must. The church must have a ministry to men if you want to reach the community holistically. Jim Ramos of Men in the Arena often says, "When a man gets it—everyone wins." I could not agree more.

But as a men's leader, you have to understand this is a calling, and it will not be easy. Many will not understand why you want to do certain activities to reach men. But just keep pursuing the call.

When you were growing up, and someone taught you how to do something, they may have gotten frustrated at some point because you didn't seem to be getting it. At some point, they may finally say, "This is not rocket science!" Well, let me tell you, Pat Morley of Man in the Mirror will tell you, ministering to men is rocket science.

I do not want to mislead you to think that ministry to men is easy and will be effective overnight when developing your leadership team. It is not, and it will not be. Richard Foster said, "Our tendency is to overestimate what we can accomplish in one year, but underestimate what we can accomplish in ten years." [13] In other words, be patient and let the Lord guide you. It takes time to build a vibrant men's ministry. Just put your faith in God and allow Him to guide you and your team as you begin to reach into men's lives.

The Call

Questions to reflect on for your next step.

- Does your church target the men of your church? If not, why not?

- How does your church select a leader for men's ministry? Does it need to change? Explain.

- Does your church décor help men to feel welcomed? What can be changed to help men feel welcomed and valuable on the church campus?

- What actions do you need to take?

Chapter 5
Discipling

Being affectionately desirous of you, we were ready to share with you not only the gospel of God but also our own selves, because you had become very dear to us.
1 Thessalonians 2:8

On the website *Church for Men*, David Murrow states,

"Men are less likely to lead, volunteer, and give in the church. They pray less, share their faith less, and read the Bible less. The men who do go to church seem passive and bored. It's often impossible to get churchgoing men to do anything other than attend services... Men need the church but, more impor-

tantly, the church needs men. The presence of enthusiastic men is one of the surest predictors of church health, growth, giving, and expansion. Meanwhile, a man shortage is a sure sign of congregational paralysis and decline." [14]

One of the reasons this is occurring in our churches is the failure to disciple men. I often tell church leaders that churches have done an excellent job in getting men to put their hands to work helping the community and those in need, especially after a disaster occurs. But as a church, we have done an equally poor job of discipling men. Discipling men help men grow in their spiritual walk and understand that faith and work go together (James 2:14-26).

Definition of Discipling

When you look up discipling in the Merriam-Webster Dictionary, you will not find the word. The online Merriam-Webster Dictionary will tell you, "The word you've entered isn't in the dictionary." [15] You will not even find the word discipling in the many translations of the Bible, but you will find the word *disciple*.

According to Merriam-Webster Dictionary, the definition of *disciple* is "one who accepts and assists in spreading the doctrines of another." [16] Also, unlike discipling, you will find the word disciple in the English Standard Version (ESV) of the Bible 28 times in the New Testament, and other translations will record it either a few times less or a few times more. You can find a few references to the word disciple in the Old Testament in other translations, particularly about being disciples of ancient kings (Is. 19:11 NIV).

Even though the word discipling is not in the Merriam-Webster Dictionary, we know it is a word. The word discipling is from the word *disciple* and the suffix *ing*. Adding the suffix makes it "an action or process" [17] happening as a disciple. The process is what Jesus was speaking about when he made the statement in Matthew 28:19, "Go… and make disciples." Use the process of discipling to make disciples.

The Greek word for our English word disciple is *mathētēs* (may-ay-tes'), which means a learner or pupil. Occasionally, people will use the word mentor as being synonymous with disciple. But are they? According to the online Merriam-Webster Dictionary, the word mentor means "a trusted counselor or guide."[18] I guess you could make the argument they mean the same. However, Jesus, His Apostles, or others God used to write the New Testament books never used the word mentor according to *Young's Analytical Concordance* [19] and *The Strongest NASB Exhaustive Concordance*.[20] These men were of the mindset to disciple those they encountered to the teachings of Jesus and the doctrines of God the Father.

Discipling or Mentoring

As a Christian, when we are discipling someone, we are teaching them to be like Christ. Paul wrote in Ephesians 5:1 to "be imitators of God." In 1 Corinthians 11:1, Paul encourages the

The Call

Corinthians to "Be imitators of me, as I am of Christ." That is the goal of discipling others in Christ—to help them become more like Christ. For us to disciple others to be more like Christ, then we need to be more like Christ.

But being a mentor is different. Being a mentor provides counsel and guidance in life journeys, taking your life experiences and using them to help others traveling a similar path you took. Not necessarily the same path but having to make similar decisions and goals to accomplish the task they have before them.

For example, I have mentors in ministering to men. One of those I have mentioned is Jeff Kisiah, Coach K as he was known. He was on the staff of a few churches as a Men's Pastor, and he instilled many of his processes, insights, and ideas to minister to men into me by coaching what it means to build an effective ministry to men. You could argue I was a disciple of his, but in this case, he was more of a mentor.

> *"Being affectionately desirous of you, we were ready to share with you not only the gospel of God but also our own selves, because you had become very dear to us."*

A verse that has had a significant impact on me to understand the importance of discipling is a statement the Apostle Paul made in one of his letters to the Thessalonians, "Being affectionately desirous of you, we were ready to share with you not only the gospel of God but also our own selves, because you had become very dear to us" (1 Thess. 2:8). He said that I am so concerned for you that I not only want to share the gospel message with you, but I want to share more. I loved you with the love of God; therefore, I want to pour my life into you. An individual exhibiting this attitude has a desire to disciple.

First Experience Being Discipled

My first experience of being discipled was with Tim Sims at Temple Baptist Church, the church I grew up in. Tim was brought on as the Youth Director when I was 16 years old. Besides having many activities, taking us to youth camps, or hanging out, he spent as much time pouring his life into us regarding how we should be walking in Christ. One of the activities we did with him that I remember the most was when he took us to the beach.

Living in a community that was just a few minutes drive to the beach, we would spend a lot of time there in the summer months. The interesting part of the trip was walking the beach with Tim sharing the gospel with people we did not know. With a couple of us standing around feeling awkward and looking lost, he would converge on these people, and share the gospel message with perfect strangers. You need to understand I was not a believer at the time, yet he still took me along.

Yes, I went to church. I grew up in church. I had walked the aisle, was baptized, and became a church member when I was thirteen years old.

The Call

As I shared in Chapter 3, my Pastor visited me when I was thirteen years old and told me it was time to join the church. He stated all my peers had joined the church, and I was one of the few in my age group who had not. He never shared the gospel message. He did not share a word of the gospel message or that I needed to surrender my life to Christ. As a current believer, I reflect on that talk and realize all he was interested in was for me to "walk the aisle," as it was known in the Baptist church, and join the membership.

During my time on the beach with Tim, I thought I was a Christian because I grew up in a Christian family, I attended church regularly, and I had "walked the aisle" to become a church member. I was on my way to being one of those church members Jesus spoke of in Matthew 7:21-23 (see Chapter 3 in this text). If something did not change, I would one day hear Jesus say, "I never knew you; depart from me, you workers of lawlessness" (Matt. 7:23).

In those days, I lacked self-confidence, and during those beach excursions, I would always try to hide behind Tim or move around where I would not be in the line of sight of those he was conversing with. I often desired to be like one of those Fiddler crabs on the beach—those tiny crabs with that one giant claw—so I could scurry into a small hole in the sand when danger is near. You probably know what I am talking about and may have experienced the same feeling in other areas of life.

I would not know what to say if I had been called upon to speak. Besides not being a believer at the time, I would only be mimicking words I had heard Tim say and not be speaking them from my heart. I suspect Tim knew that. He was praying that through this experience, those he took with him would see the grace of God and the gift of eternal life God was offering each one of us if we would just accept the gift.

If we were not on the beach, we would spend many weekend nights in the Coffee House that Temple Baptist had for the youth in those days. For your information, Coffee Houses back then were nothing like today's coffee houses. For one thing—they did not sell coffee. There probably was not even any coffee in the house! They didn't sell anything. In fact, I do not even know why it was called a Coffee House back then. It was a place for youth to hang out, play pool, ping-pong, or any number of other pastimes. Tim would spend many of those nights sharing verses from Romans, he called the Roman Road. As he did, the verses began to find residence within many of us, including myself.

The Decision

One night I was in my bedroom lying on my bed reading the Roman Road verses and thinking about what Tim had told us about each one when I felt the tug of the Holy Spirit upon my life. For some reason, I cannot tell you why, other than the Holy Spirit encouraging me.

Over against the wall in my room, there was a straight back chair that was older than me. My parents had probably owned it since the day they were married. Over the years, the chair had become worn and tattered, and Mom had made a blue slip-cover to put over it. I got up from my bed and walked over, and knelt beside the chair. Using the chair as my altar, I accepted God's gift of eternal life by surrendering my life to Christ on a January night in 1972.

I do not know what happened to the chair, but now, almost 50 years later, I wish I had that chair. Why? Because the chair is a life marker. It is like the stone Jacob placed to mark his encounter with God at Bethel (Gen. 29:17-22). Or the pillow of stones Joshua had the Israelites erect when they crossed the Jordan as they entered the Promised Land to remind future generations what God had done (Joshua 4:1-24). It is a marker I could have used to tell my kids and grandkids why I still had the chair. It is where I encountered God for the first time.

Discipling Changed Many Lives

Tim was a discipler to teenagers in the early 1970s. He lived over the Coffee House on Temple Baptist Church campus, and we could visit him anytime, even at 2:00 am. Tim always had time to listen and share our lives. After I went to college, I lost touch with him as he resigned from his position at Temple and moved on to other God-appointed opportunities.

This discipling relationship Tim developed with me started with me not being a child of God. Several of us in the group were not believers when Tim began to disciple us. But it was through his discipling, pouring his life into us, that resulted in many of us coming to Christ in our teenage years. If you have not picked up on it, the point I am making is that you can disciple people who are not believers hoping they will come to Christ. Jesus did this. At the beginning of His ministry, he came up to men of various walks of life and said, "Follow me."

Follow Me

These men may have known of Jesus and his ministry, but at first, they did not know he was the Son of God and that He would die for their sins. They probably liked what they heard, and when Jesus came and gave them a personal invitation to join Him on His journey, they readily accepted.

Now you may or may not be able to come up to someone and say, "Follow me," but you can encourage those who are not believers to join you for breakfast or lunch or invite them to attend an event with you so you can begin a discipling relationship. Some of these men that Jesus asked may have known Him because of His reputation of traveling the region performing miracles.

In the first 50 years of attending church, the relationship I had with Tim is the only one I can say that emulated a discipling relationship. Even then, I did not realize what Tim was doing. It was never described as a discipling relationship. He was a youth leader hanging with teenagers, sometimes as a group, sometimes individually pouring his life into them, teaching them how to follow Christ. Years later, I learned from my mentor, Jeff Kisiah, as I began to minister to men; it is called The Ministry of Hanging Out.

The Ministry of Hanging Out

The Ministry of Hanging Out is connecting with friends and acquaintances to build relationships to provide encouragement and possibly let those who have not accepted God's gift of eternal life see Jesus through those who have—leading to a discipling relationship. The ministry of hanging out can be seen in activities such as cookouts, hunting, fishing, attending ballgames, or any number of activities where men hang out to fellowship.

Go And Make Disciples

It would be 35 years before I understood a real discipling relationship. Being in church, attending Bible studies, Sunday School, and conferences, I would hear about being a disciple of Christ, but never was there a description of one man pouring his life into another in a discipling relationship. Not until I was dealing with my cancer and God speaking to me in so many ways did I begin to understand that it was a command for me to disciple others as a believer.

I had heard about going and making disciples about which Jesus spoke in Matthew 28:19, but I thought, because this is what I was taught, I was to witness to those who cross my path, encourage them to pray the sinner's prayer, and then welcome them into the family of God. Never in my wildest dreams was I taught or did I understand I should also take them under my wing and pour my life into these people or help them get into a discipling relationship if I could not personally help them grow in Christ.

The Bible is straightforward in that we are to pour our lives into others in discipling relationships. Let these verses speak to you. Words underlined are mine.

1 Thessalonians 2:8— So, being affectionately desirous of you, we were ready to share with you not only the gospel of God <u>but also our own selves</u>, because you had become very dear to us.

Matthew 28:19-20— Go therefore and <u>make disciples of all nations</u>, baptizing them in the name of the Father and of the Son and of the Holy Spirit, teaching them to observe all that I have commanded you.

2 Timothy 2:1-2— You then, my child, be strengthened by the grace that is in Christ Jesus, and <u>what you have heard from me in the presence of many witnesses entrust to faithful men who will be able to teach others also</u>.

Act 1:8— But you will receive power when the Holy Spirit has come upon you, and <u>you will be my witnesses</u> in Jerusalem and in all Judea and Samaria, and to the end of the earth."

Romans 10:14-15— How then will they call on him in whom they have not believed? And how are they to believe in him of whom they have never heard? <u>And how are they to hear without someone preaching</u>? And how are they to preach unless they are sent?

As it is written, "How beautiful are the feet of those who preach the good news!"

Colossians 1:28-29— Him we proclaim, <u>warning everyone and teaching everyone with all wisdom</u>, that we may present everyone mature in Christ. For this I toil, struggling with all his energy that he powerfully works within me.

Disciple Your Family

It is essential that as a man, you are a discipler. Your first responsibility is to disciple your family, letting your children see you spending time reading the Bible and praying. Then spend time pouring your life spiritually into your children, teaching them how to read the Bible and pray. God expected the Israelite Dads to pour into their children's lives, and we should today. Listen to these words from Deuteronomy 6:4-7 as you read this scripture.

"Hear, O Israel: The LORD our God, the LORD is one. You shall love the LORD your God with all your heart and with all your soul and with all your might. And these words that I command you today shall be on your heart. You shall teach them diligently to your children, and shall talk of them when you sit in your house, and when you walk by the way, and when you lie down, and when you rise."

In case you didn't see it, we are to talk to our children in every part of the day, no matter what we are doing about the things of God—teaching them to love God with all their heart, soul, and might.

Then you need to seek someone for you to disciple outside your family. Ask God to reveal someone for you to walk up to and intentionally ask them to follow you. Now you may not say "follow me," but it may all begin with asking them to have breakfast, lunch, or just a cup of coffee.

Make Discipling a Life Habit

Once the word is out that you are a discipler, you need to be ready for men to approach you and ask you to disciple them. One such time a man from the church I was attending asked if I would meet with him. I agreed, and we met at a local fast-food restaurant for breakfast. During this meeting, he shared he wanted someone to help him grow in Christ. After some more discussion, I agreed to meet with him weekly. I met with him for a year.

> *Let your pastor, other staff members, and your men's leader know you are available to disciple.*

What was interesting in this relationship is that he kept asking if he could bring others to join us. As long as the group size was no more than four, including me, I would agree. Some would stay a few weeks, and others would be there for the long haul.

I have had church leaders reach out to me and ask if I would meet with college students. I always said yes if I had the time, but I would encourage the individuals to have the candidate contact me.

Let your pastor, other staff members, and your men's leader know you are available to disciple. They will be happy to steer individuals in your direction, and it will be an encouragement to them.

Discipled Men Minister to Others

Many men who are active in the church generally desire to reach out and help individuals in need. Many of the men in our churches are involved in helping with maintenance activities around the church. They are helping with a recovery effort after a devastating storm has come through an area. They might be involved in building ramps to provide accessibility for the disabled to their homes. The men may even go on various types of mission trips.

In my travels, I have seen men working hard to deal with an individual's specific needs. They may have been trained to do the task assigned, and they do an exceptional job. But there is another aspect that equips men to minister to the spiritual needs of the individual.

When men are involved in being discipled, this will help them be equipped to minister more effectively. Generally, men who are in discipling relationships will be the first to volunteer for missional opportunities.

Men are often trained in specific tasks. However, most men have not been discipled to grow spiritually, to share the gospel, pray with and for someone, or how to respond when people ask you, "Why?" Men like helping the physical needs but often lack the skills to deal with the spiritual needs.

When on a mission project, we encourage team members to develop a relationship with the ministered person. Not everyone on the team will be able to do this; but, someone in the group may be able to relate with the one being ministered to. Take the time to get to know them and, at some point, talk with them about spiritual matters.

I have noticed men who have been in discipling relationships are more likely to develop those relationships with others. Therefore, it is essential to help move our men into discipling relationships to develop the spiritual maturity to speak into others' lives.

As men grow spiritually in their walk with God, they will develop the confidence to speak into people's lives. There is a direct correlation between growing men in spiritual maturity and moving men into mission projects.

As you evaluate your church's ministry to men, check to be sure you are not only training them to perform specific tasks exceptionally well, but the ministry is also discipling the men so they can speak into others' lives with confidence.

Being a discipler is a command of the Lord. As a leader of men, you need to be discipling other men. You need to die to yourself and put yourself out there to help men grow in Christ.

The Purpose of Ministering to Men

A lot of churches use the verse from Proverbs as their men's ministry verse. "As iron sharpens iron, and one man sharpens another" (Pro. 27:17). But for this to happen, a man must have another man in his life. Ecclesiastes 4:9-12 explains what that means.

Two are better than one, because they have a good reward for their toil. For if they fall, one will lift up his fellow. But woe to him who is alone when he falls and has not another to lift him up! Again, if two lie together, they keep warm, but how can one keep warm alone? And though a man might prevail against one who is alone, two will withstand him—a threefold cord is not quickly broken.

A man must have another man for him to be sharpened like iron is sharpened.

Many Christian men start with a passion for the things of God but then begin to coast. They end up compromising, and many finish their lives with regret. In his book *Every Man A Warrior: Helping Men Succeed In Life—Walking with God*, Lonnie Berger states, "I believe that most men have never been trained and equipped with the necessary skills to fight and end well." [21] In his book *Often Told Rarely Trained*, Dale Forehand made this statement, "I believe that for way too much of my Christian life, I had the testimony of being often told, rarely trained." [22] If we are honest with ourselves, most of us could say the same thing.

As we minister to men, part of our men's ministry should be to move men into discipling relationships. This is more than being in church on Sunday morning and attending a Sunday School class or a Home Group Study. All of these are important, and every man should be attending these with their wife and family. Even a single man should be actively engaged in attending some biblical study. But the relationship I am talking about is placing oneself in a position so a man can pour his life into us. Creating an environment where men feel comfortable to discuss issues and struggles they deal with every day.

Some of the most meaningful times I have experienced in the last decade of my walk with God is spending time with 2–3 other men to dig deep into the scriptures, discuss how to apply them into my life, and allowing those men to speak into my life.

Start A Discipling Group

For 35 years as a Christian, I limped along, trying to advance my walk in Christ by myself and never developing a relationship with other men. Men who I had permitted to speak into my life— to speak truth into my life, to encourage—genuine encouragement and not the superficial encouragement we often hear from those just outside the boundaries we set up.

To move men to spiritual maturity, we need to develop an attitude of moving men into discipling relationships. How do we do that? Invite them to join you in working through a book or a book of the Bible. It's not hard. I have found a great book to start with is by Dr. Gary Yagel called, *Got Your Back*. It is an easy read, and it is a great book to help men understand why we need other men in our lives.

As someone once said, "Discipleship is the answer to our evangelism problem." Men who we invite into our group do not need to be Christians. One can use these groups to develop relationships to present the gospel in a comfortable and non-threatening environment to those who do not know Christ. I was not a Christian when Tim Sims began discipling me.

In Chapter 4, I made a statement that we are in the battle for men's souls. Discipling is how we fight this battle. One man at a time. One man committing his life to go and make disciples (Matt. 28:19), inviting another man to take a journey with him on an adventure that will be exciting and encouraging for that man to be the man God desires.

Paul made it personal by telling the Thessalonians in his first letter to them, "We cared so much for you that we were pleased to share with you not only the gospel of God but also our own lives, because you had become dear to us" (1 Th 2:8).

So, if you want to move your men's ministry deeper to reach the men of your church and community, start by moving men into spiritual maturity by developing a discipling ministry. As a seasoned man once told me after experiencing a few weeks in a discipleship group, "This is the best thing I have experienced since I became a Christian!"

Questions to reflect on for your next step.

- Have you ever been in a discipleship group? If not, why?

- Do you feel you have often been told but rarely trained? What can you do about it?

- Do you feel every man should either be discipled or be the discipler or both? Explain.

- What actions do you need to take?

The Call

Chapter 6
Invite Someone to Take a Journey

"Follow Me."

Matthew 4:19

All of us like to take journeys. Some may go on trips across their state. Others across the country. Even others to other countries. I have known people who cruise along the eastern seaboard and others who go on 30-45 day world trips. I am not a world traveler, and I am not one to trek across the country just to visit sites. But I am on a journey, and occasionally, I will invite a man to take the journey with me. These are times when I reach out and intentionally invite a man on a spiritual journey.

Intentionality

I was teaching a Men's Ministry Leadership class in Asheville, NC, a few years back, when I began to talk about being intentional in their ministry. I had a man ask me, "What do you mean by being intentional?" That is a great question, and we are going to unpack what it means to be intentional in this chapter. It is a process I had never heard used when ministering to men until a decade ago when I met my men's ministry leadership mentor, Jeff Kisiah.

The root word for intentional is *intend*, and the Merriam-Webster Dictionary defines it as "to have in mind as a purpose or goal or plan." Merriam-Webster defines *intentional* as "done by intention or design." Therefore, to be *intentional* regarding ministering to men means you are reaching out to your men with a purpose and plan in mind. But for me to help you understand what intentional looks like in action, I need to share some instances in the Bible and life experiences.

Jesus was Intentional

There are a few events that come to mind in the Bible when I think of displays of intentionality. One is when Jesus was walking by the Sea of Galilee, and he saw Simon (Peter) and his brother

Andrew, and he said to them, "Follow me, and I will make you fishers of men" (Matt. 4:19). Jesus intentionally reached out to Simon and Andrew, inviting them to take a journey with Him, walk with Him, and allow Him to speak into their lives.

A short time later, Jesus encountered Matthew, a tax collector, one who was in one of the most hated positions in Israel of the day. Generally, a tax collector was a Jew who had betrayed his people to work with the Roman government to collect taxes—usually much more than required to supplement his income. Jesus saw him and said, "Follow me" (Mat. 9:9). Matthew had likely witnessed Jesus' public teaching and healings and was now ready to join Him.

The scriptures then tell us that Jesus went a little farther and saw James and his brother John mending the nets. Jesus called them, and they left the boat with the hired servants and followed Him (Mk 1:19-20). Later, Jesus spent the night praying, and as a result, He called 12 of His disciples and named them apostles to join Him on the journey He was taking (Luke 6:12-16). Jesus had a plan for those men. As you read through the Gospels and into the book Acts of the Apostles, you see that plan coming to fruition.

Tapping on the Shoulder

The Bible indicates Jesus called each of these men by name and essentially tapped them on the shoulder and said, "Follow Me."

The Call

Several times in the gospels, we read of Jesus tapping on the shoulder of Peter, James, and John to accompany Him on a particular task (Mat. 17:1; Mar. 5:37; Mar. 14:33; Luk 8:51). He was permitting only them to be a participant in an event He wanted them to experience as He prepared them for the ministry to which He was calling them.

The most obvious tapping of the shoulder is when Jesus appeared to Saul on the road to Damascus to question Saul as why he was persecuting Him. Saul knew who he was speaking with as he referred to Jesus as Lord (Acts 9:5). Jesus instructed Saul, who we now know through the rest of the New Testament as Paul, to continue on his journey to Damascus, and there he would be told what to do (Acts 9:6).

Each of these is a display of Jesus being intentional. He essentially tapped individuals on the shoulder of those He wanted to pour His life into to prepare them for the ministry He was calling them. When I look at Jesus, I see intentionality. In his book *Mentor Like Jesus*, Regi Campbell stated that Jesus didn't have time for His disciples just to show up. He had to go and get them.[23] We do not need to live a life thinking men will come running for us to speak into their lives. If Jesus reached out to men of His time to pour His life into them, what makes us think that we do not need to do the same. Especially with the attitude and the hustling and bustling of the culture of today.

We have to understand that going to a church service once a week is not discipling. Attending a Sunday School class is a type of discipling, but we desire a man to spend one-on-one time with a few men pouring his life into them.

"Tapping them on the shoulder" is a metaphor of personally inviting an individual to join you in a discipling relationship or inviting them to join you at an event or gathering where they would be encouraged into a discipling relationship.

The Mission

By Jesus' example, we can transfer that to the calling God has placed on all our lives to "Go… and make disciples." We must be intentional in our mission of making disciples. They do not just come to us. A few may approach us on their own, but most will not. So, we must invite them on the journey just like Jesus did and is still doing. I have experienced this in my own life. I have been tapped on the shoulder, and I have tapped others on the shoulder. Let me share a few.

Many years ago, I talked with a few people after church when Mr. Tommy walked up to me and asked me if I would be interested in attending a Bible study with a few men on Saturday mornings at 6:00 am. I wrote about this in Chapter 2. After a few minutes of discussion with Mr. Tommy, I accepted. I participated in that group for the next three years, and it radically changed my life. I grew more in those three years than I had in all the years before since I became a believer. Through that experience, I gained a new perspective of what it meant to disciple someone else, and I learned what Jesus meant when He commanded us to "Go… and make disciples."

The Call

I need to say this was the first time I had experienced being in a men's only study where I felt I could share thoughts and feelings that I could not share in coed classes. Before this time in my life, I did not know these groups existed. Why? Because I never was invited. Though I know now as a men's leader, many of these groups were happening.

> *Do not ever assume that someone is in a group. The only way to know for sure is to ask.*

No man had stepped up and intentionally invited me to join a group. It could have been because I was so active in church; men who were, if they were, involved in discipleship groups may have thought I was already in a group. Do not ever assume that someone is in a group. The only way to know for sure is to ask.

We think we can make announcements on the platform or in the bulletin, and men will get the message and come running to join. Not so. Most men tune out the announcements or do not read the bulletin. If they do hear the announcement, they blow it off as that is not for me. You must intentionally invite the man to join you on the journey.

Now understand, I am not saying never make a verbal announcement from the platform or place a notice in the bulletin. I highly recommend that you do make announcements and put information in bulletins because you very well may reach a man. I just want you to understand the most effective method to get men involved is personally inviting them to join you.

Seek God in the Process

I learned to apply Jesus' method by praying about who I should tap on the shoulder from this experience. When I did, God led me to other men I reached out to and tapped them on the shoulder and personally asked them if they would be willing to meet with me to study God's Word or work through a book to help enhance spiritual growth. Most of the men that have participated have shared how important this became to them, all because I did what Jesus modeled by reaching out and being intentional to individuals He led me to.

Intentional Definition

So, what does it mean to be intentional? It means inviting someone to take a journey with you to grow spiritually, so they will understand what Jesus meant when he said: "Go... and make disciples." It can also mean to invite someone to an event or gathering that might result in the Holy Spirit prompting them to seek a man or group of men to join on a spiritual journey.

As I shared in Chapter 4, Tim Sims introduced me to being discipled though I did not understand the process at the time. He intentionally poured his life into several other teenagers and me to help us understand God's saving grace and develop a relationship with Jesus. Through Tim's intentionality, I came to Christ.

You can be intentional with believers and non-believers. Each has its merit for being intentional. Tim discipling me was my first experience of seeing someone being intentional. But I only recognize this as I reflect on my life before Christ and immediately after surrendering to Christ.

Practicing Intentionality

We need to understand there are many ways to be intentional, like men gathering together on a ball field to attending retreats and conferences and inviting a man out to breakfast or lunch and paying for their meal. Praying with them when they ask for prayer is intentional. Don't just say you will remember them in prayer but pray for them right then and there. At every step, the intention is to help them become the men God created them to be.

I had a friend who purchased college football tickets, and he would always buy one more. Why? So he could invite a man to attend with him and use the time to pour his life into that man. That is being intentional. I knew another who used to purchase extra NASCAR racing tickets to invite a man to attend with him to develop that discipling relationship. That is being intentional.

There are so many ways one can be intentional with men. On the website *IntentionalWay.org*, Jeff Kisiah stated that intentionality is,

- Defined as "done by intent or design."
- Differentiated by both advance planning and spontaneous reactions.

A Journey Into Men's Ministry

- Designed to live your life and minister to others in a very purposeful way.
- Devoting necessary time and energy to leave the world a better place.

He also stated, "There are many ways to practice Intentionality. It should be part of your personal life, family life, and ministry life." Most discipling groups are begun by one man being intentional, reaching out by tapping men on the shoulder.

When men get together, intentionality is in play, whether it is a planned event or a spontaneous gathering. It would help if you used these times to get to know the men. Using these gathering times to know the men will help you understand those who need to be in discipling relationships. We discuss this more in Chapter 7.

A Discipleship Group

A few years ago, I felt led to start a men's discipleship group with the men in the couple's class I teach on Sunday mornings. After researching, which included much prayer, I settled on the book *Got Your Back* by Gary Yagel to begin this group. I chose this book because it provides insight into why men need to have other men in their lives. In his book, Gary had a quote from Stu Weber from Stu's days in Army Ranger School, which hit me square between the eyes. Gary quoted Stu recounting the words of his C.O. at the Army Ranger School as saying,

The Call

"Step one in your training is the assignment of your 'Ranger Buddy.' Difficult assignments require a friend. The two of you will stick together. You will never leave each other. You will walk together, run together, eat together, and sleep together. You will help each other. You will encourage each other. And as necessary, you will carry each other."[25]

What can be more difficult in our lives than to live a life as a follower of Christ. We need men to be our "spiritual buddy."

I also planned to have the group meet at my house at 9:00 am Wednesday since they are retired. I also wanted to keep the group no larger than five men, including myself.

After working through the group meeting logistics, I now had to invite the men to attend, tapping them on the shoulder to join me on this journey. There were four men in the class I planned to ask. I did not want to send them an email or make a phone call; though I could have done either, I wanted to invite them face-to-face. I wanted the men to understand the importance I placed on these groups, so I intentionally invited these men face-to-face. Asking the men with a face-to-face meeting is what I would encourage you to do when planning your discipleship group or if you are going to disciple one man.

Though there may be times you will need to converse by email, text, or phone calls, your initial contact should be a face-to-face meeting. If the men you desire to invite to your group are not in a class like mine in this example, ask them to a breakfast or lunch meeting or maybe meet at a coffee shop. But whatever you do, try to meet the men face-to-face. Meeting face-to-face will indicate to them the importance you place on the group and care about their spiritual development.

I invited the men in my group during the fellowship time before calling the class together to start. I spoke to each one individually, explaining the idea for the group. To my delight, each man I approached said yes. Now I had an advantage with these men because they already knew me. I was not someone they see in church or the neighborhood from time to time or even a stranger. These men knew me. They had sat under my teaching for a time, so they were my friends. But understand that not all friends will be ready to make such a commitment.

So how did I explain the idea of the group, and how did I get them to agree?

As I said earlier, I approached each man individually. I told them I wanted to invite them to meet with me weekly to walk through the book *Got Your Back*. But before they gave me an answer, I provided them an out if they would agree to meet. I stated if they committed four weeks to me, I would commit to them that at that time, all they would have to do is tell me that this is not for them, and they could walk away with no questions. They all agreed to the conditions. If you provide certain conditions, be sure you follow through.

Shortly afterward, we started meeting. Each one of the men attended faithfully for the four weeks. At the end of the fourth meeting, I thanked them for being faithful in their attendance and commitment. Now I would honor my commitment by stating that if this was not what any of them expected or if they felt it was not for them, they should just let me know that they did not want to continue to attend, and there would be no questions. None of the men were ready to quit; all wanted to continue. One said he never experienced anything like this in his 40 years of being in the church. He was in it for the long haul.

Iron Sharpens Iron

Most men's ministries use Proverbs 27:17, "As iron sharpens iron, so one man sharpens another" (NIV), as the ministry verse. Have you thought about what that means? What happens when two iron rods or flat bars rub together?

In my days as an industrial mechanic in the power industry, I had the privilege to open a gearbox that had failed. Sometimes we would find that a retainer ring or bushing had failed and allowed two rotating gears to begin rubbing together. The metals begin to create heat which softens the metal and begins to remove metal particles. As this continues, the metals start to become smooth and begin to shine. Eventually, the metals will sharpen and will become sharp as razors if allowed to go long enough.

Iron sharpens iron is an analogy of two men sharpening each other. As Stu Weber's C.O. in his Army Ranger School stated, they will begin to sharpen each other as they work together. They will start to knock off the rough edges as they pray and encourage each other. They will help each other hide the Word of God in their hearts and begin to shine as the image of Christ as He begins to show through the men.

Then just as the scripture teaches that the Word of God is sharper than a two-edged sword, the men's thoughts and attitudes of the heart (Heb. 4:12) will be changed into men who will go and make disciples. They will become husbands who honor their wives (1 Pet. 3:7) and dads who will teach their children diligently in the things of God (Deut. 6:7).

The group I spoke of above has been meeting now for three years. In that time, two left to begin their own group, and we have added two other men. Even during the COVID-19 pandemic, we learned to use video technology to conduct our meetings when we could not meet face-to-face. Though it is not the same, it still maintained the camaraderie of the group.

All of us are called and commanded to make disciples. Begin praying today for God to lead you to those whom you can tap on the shoulder and be intentional by inviting them on a journey to grow closer to God. You will be blessed and discover many rewards in your own life when you do.

The Call

Questions to reflect on for your next step.

- What are your thoughts on Stu Weber's comment about a Ranger Buddy in the format as a Christian brother having your back?

- Have you ever been tapped on the shoulder, or have you ever tapped someone on the shoulder?

- Would you like to be tapped on the shoulder if you haven't?

- What actions do you need to take?

Chapter 7
How To Get Men Involved

Two are better than one, because they have a good reward for their toil. For if they fall, one will lift up his fellow. But woe to him who is alone when he falls and has not another to lift him up!
Ecclesiastes 4:9-10

In the last chapter, we talked about being intentional in your approach to speaking into men's lives. We need to be intentional, so we can help men connect with other men, and as leaders, we can get to know them. This chapter covers two other areas my men's ministry mentor spoke into me regularly regarding developing your ministry to men: creating multiple entry points and knowing your men.

There are four areas most churches lack to support a ministry to men: Lack of Leadership, Lack of Promotion, Lack of Masculine Presence, we discussed in earlier chapters. The fourth one is a Lack of Finances.

Lack of Finances

Suppose you take time to study your church's budget. In that case, you will probably find that men's ministry is the least financial commitment of any other ministry, sometimes less than the flower budget for putting flowers on the altar table for Sunday services. In some churches, men's ministry is not even a line item in the church budget.

The reason given most of the time is that men can cover the cost of the activity. Churches are blind to how gatherings and events designed explicitly for men can create the next right step for them to take on the road to discipleship. The goal is to encourage growing spiritually in their walk with Christ, becoming better leaders, husbands, and dads. Give serious consideration if the men's ministry budget is adequate or needs to be increased.

Entry Points

Creating entry points and knowing your church's men is necessary to reach every man in your church. I will submit to you that if you are not thinking about reaching every man in your church and operating as every man in your church is a part of the ministry to men, your group will become nothing more than a social gathering.

When you think about your men's entry points, I have found three areas your leadership team needs to consider: events, spiritual growth opportunities, and mission opportunities. To get to know them, I found three additional practices to help: talk with the men, meet with a man individually, and surveys. As the leadership team learns the interest, hobbies, struggles, and spiritual maturity of the men, you will be able to plan the entry points adequately.

Let's begin to unpack these areas we need to incorporate in our ministry to men to develop that effective and vibrant ministry. First, we will look at the entry points.

Everybody enjoys a good event. Before we get into the discussion on entry points, I need to remind you that events are created to help men take the next right step into discipling relationships, as we stated in Chapter 5. Yes, time of fellowship and having a good time is part of the event, but the main focus on the leadership team is to use these event activities to help men move into discipling relationships.

The number of events you schedule and plan for your men each year will depend on your church's size and the number of men in your church. A vibrant ministry to men will generally have at least four events each year—one per quarter—but no less than two events each year.

The Call

Regardless of the number of men in your church, your men's ministry leadership team should plan a different activity each quarter. Why? You want to create events that will, over some time, resonate with the interest of every man in the church.

It is essential to have a men's ministry leadership team to develop various events or gatherings. The team should include men who have a diverse set of interests. This way, one man does not plan all events. If a single leader leads your men's ministry, there is a good chance the leader will prepare all the gatherings around his interest. A leadership team with men of diverse interests will have more success in planning events that will appeal to more men.

> *It is essential to have a men's ministry leadership team to develop various events or gatherings.*

Some examples of men's events many churches have planned are a Wild Game Night, a golf scramble, a NASCAR or some other sport watch party, a car show, a trip to a ball game, a father/son outing, or even a hatchet-throwing contest. Having a different event each quarter will show the team's desire to connect with all the men in the church and not just a select few.

Each event should involve a spiritual element, such as devotion, testimony, or speaker. Let me say one thing about the time limit. Whatever you do, please make sure the person speaking understands they are on a time limit—no more than fifteen minutes, and the speaker has a message that will connect with the men. You do not want to bore your men to the point they begin to leave, or when the next event is scheduled, they remember the previous long speaker and decide to forgo the event.

Speaker Expectations

Several years ago, a church invited me to attend a men's cookout as a guest. It was a great time of fellowship and games until the guest speaker began to speak. He spoke for an hour. I watched men leave, and to be honest, I was tempted to leave. I watched as men began to look at their wristwatches and started checking messages on their phones. The speaker was rambling and was not connecting with the men.

Events should encourage men in their spiritual growth and to become involved in spiritual growth groups. In the book *How to Disciple Men*, Truett Wayne Pool Jr. writes, "I encourage you to see the value of each event from several perspectives. That includes team building, leadership training, a chance to help some of your men step out of their comfort zone, evangelism training, positive partnership with other ministries in your church, outreach to pew sitters, outreach to the community, connecting generations, and even, maybe, launching a new dimension to your men's ministry, such as a small groups or a handyman ministry." [26]

Be careful who you have as a guest speaker and the length of time they speak. If they are long-winded, I would advise not to use them unless they can be trusted to end at a specific time.

Conferences

Another type of entry point is to invite men to attend a men's conference your church plans to attend. But why would a man want to attend a men's conference? To answer that question, one needs to understand the purpose of a men's conference and the types of conferences available.

All men's conferences are designed to encourage men to be the men God created them to be; but, not all men's conferences are created equal. Conferences are developed from many different perspectives. For example, some are designed as an evangelistic conference or focuses on men's particular interests. Some conferences attract the younger generation, and some are more suited for the older generation. Some conferences focus on a specific interest, such as a man who is an outdoorsman. Then some conferences are built around the keynote speaker.

There are many different styles and types of conferences men can choose to attend. However, I believe there is one type of conference that can connect with every man in your church, and that is an equipping conference.

An equipping conference does not limit itself to a particular subject or built around a keynote speaker. An equipping conference is designed for men of all ages and at various places in their life. At an equipping conference, men hear from leaders speaking on multiple subjects that can help them spiritually grow and help them speak into their family's lives or other men's lives.

A Journey Into Men's Ministry

Men have the opportunity to attend breakout sessions to hear experts in their field speak on subjects such as discipling, addictions, participate in sessions dealing with being a husband, father, and grandfather—often called tune-ups. They can attend sessions on developing a men's ministry in your church or maintaining it, or getting men involved in mission projects. There can even be sessions discussing what to do after retirement to help your church or community and many other subjects. The list could be extensive.

An equipping conference allows men to discover the many resources available to help churches reach the men in their respective churches and community. Men will have opportunities to speak and ask questions of these leaders, developing a relationship. One of the areas I struggled with greatly when I became the men's leader at my church was finding resources and discovering experts in the men's ministry field to help and mentor. I had no idea of the amount of material available. Through an equipping conference, you can discover these resources.

As you plan your next conference experience be sure to consider the type of conference that would best benefit your men. Which experience would help your men the most and provide resources and connections that will continue for months, even years to come. If you choose the right conference for your men, the ones who attend will be the best to get the word out and encourage men to attend the next one.

Tom Chesire of Relevant Practical Ministry for Men discusses attending a men's conference regardless of the type: "There's no better way to build relational capital with your guys."[27]

The Call

Spiritual Growth

The next area the men's ministry leadership team needs to address is spiritual growth.

I once heard a pastor state he needs to take a few months to evaluate what is most effective to reach men: discipleship groups, Bible study groups, events, or men's conferences. Each one is as effective as the other and should be incorporated to reach all the church and community men. Why? Because each one of these methods will reach the man where he is in his spiritual walk.

In their book *No Man Left Behind,* Man in the Mirror states there are five types of men in the church: a Lost Man, a Cultural Christian, a Biblical Christian, a Leader, and all across the other four are Hurting Men.[28] Each of the methods the pastor said he must evaluate will be effective in reaching those men differently.

Even if a man does not realize he is spiritually lost, a man who does not have a relationship with Christ will probably not attend a discipleship group. However, suppose they are regular attenders of the church. In that case, they might attend a Bible study group, and they will likely participate in a men's activity event or even a mission opportunity. Besides, successful discipleship groups generally are created by someone intentionally inviting a man to attend, as discussed in the last chapter.

In Bible Study Groups, there is a camaraderie that develops between men. They enjoy meeting together and listening to someone speak into their lives without having to be transparent or vulnerable. They may not even need to be accountable to anyone. But the time together encourages the men.

Men's activity events are opportunities to allow them to hear testimonies through either planned talks or conversations about men involved in Bible study groups, discipleship groups, and missional activities. God can use these discussions to capture a man's heart and draw his interest to be involved in one of these groups. Eventually, the Holy Spirit will tug at his heart enough that either he will seek a group or when someone taps him on the shoulder to invite him to a group, he will accept.

I discussed men's conferences above, but I want to mention them again to encourage as a tool for spiritual growth and work much like a local church men's event. I do classify men's conferences as two different types: Pep Rally or Equipping. Nothing wrong with either one, and each has a place in ministering to men. Attending a pep rally type conference, a man will hear good speakers and music. The men are encouraged and are around like-minded men, but it has been my experience that for most men, in a few days to a week after returning, the excitement has vanished, and in two to three weeks, it is back to everyday life before the conference.

Men attending an equipping conference are provided tools to take back home and apply to their daily life. They can choose seminars, or as often called, breakout sessions, to attend, which resonate with them.

Mission Opportunities

Another process the leadership team can use to create entry points for the men is through mission opportunities.

By participating in mission projects, men will build relationships by putting their hands and feet to work. These mission opportunities can be anything from yard projects to disaster relief. While the men are working together and getting to know one another, among the many conversations they will have, some will eventually turn to discuss being in a discipleship group. This may even result in men inviting other men to join.

Being involved in mission opportunities can also lead to meeting men who are spiritually lost. Seeing men putting their faith to work by meeting others' needs will open doors of opportunities to share the gospel message.

Men in spiritual growth groups will be looking for opportunities in the missional area as they grow in their walk with Christ. Be sure that you include missional opportunities as part of your entry points. Not all men will be growing in Christ, but many will have a compassion to help others in need. This will open opportunities to encourage men into groups studying God's Word to grow and become the man God designed him to be.

One final encouragement regarding the leadership's mission opportunities is to be sure you work with your church's mission pastor or mission leader to discover opportunities for your men to be involved.

Men's Ministry Goal

As we stated earlier in this chapter, not all men are created equal. Each man is at a different point in his life and in his spiritual walk. Some are ready to dive into deep studies of the Word; others are interested in being a part of a small discipleship group, while others are just fine right now to gather together in social settings. The ultimate goal of any ministry to men is to move men into discipling relationships in which they will eventually step out and disciple other men.

Know Your Men

To help men connect with a discipleship group, we need to know the men connected with the local church. Remember, we stated that when dealing with the church's men, the leadership team needs to consider all men connected with your church as part of your ministry to men.

To plan the right events or studies, you must know the men—the man. Like a former basketball coach once told me, he had to know his players to develop a championship team. He had to understand their skills and talent in the sport and what they bring to the game so he could assemble them into a highly efficient and effective basketball team. He had to know his players. Now we are not developing a basketball team, but we are developing a team of men who will be the image-bearers of Christ in this world we live.

The Call

How did the coach get to know his players? He observed them during practice, watching their skills and how they interacted with the other players, he talked with them as a group, and he spoke with them individually. We may not be able to do all the coach did to observe the men in the church, but we can use some of the ideas and recognize other ways to get to know our men.

Here are some techniques and thoughts on how to get to know our men.

Talk With The Men

The best way is just to talk with the men. Notice I said talk *with* and not talk *to*. You want to get to know them. When one talks to someone, they are the ones doing most of the talking. But here you want them to talk to you. During a breakfast or dinner gathering or some other time you have a group of men together, ask some open-ended questions to get them to start talking. But once they do, you may learn a lot. You want them to share their lives, interests, careers, hobbies, and struggles. Make sure you take some discreet notes while everyone is sharing. Maybe get one of your leadership team members to take notes so the team can review what was said later as you plan future events and studies. One

> *When one talks to someone, they are the ones doing most of the talking.*

important consideration of your note-taking—NO NAMES—just the comments.

Barnabas Lunch Appointments

My mentor, Jeff Kisiah, was big on what he called Barnabas Lunch Appointments (BLA). He instilled this in me as he mentored me, and I use it even as a state and regional leader to help understand the needs of men and men leaders. These appointments are nothing more than intentionally planning a lunch meeting with a man to get to know or encourage him individually. To my knowledge, Jeff is  the one that coined the phrase. I have never heard anyone else use this phrase unless Jeff mentored them. When Jeff said he had a BLA, you knew what he was doing. He was going to meet another man to spend some time and fellowship with him.

He taught me the importance of just sitting across a table from another man, breaking bread together, and talking. He believed he could learn a lot about the man and his needs during these times more than anything else he could do. You may not be able to meet with every man in your church, but with your

The Call

leadership team's help, you could make a big dent in meeting your men over time.

Here is an interesting note. A BLA can be a catalyst to move a man into a discipling relationship. As you meet regularly with the man and learn more about him, you can provide material to help him grow spiritually and as a leader.

Through this, you will be astonished by what you will learn. You can also let a BLA evolve into inviting a man to attend a sporting event or work with you on a project or hobby. Do not let these BLAs be a one-time meeting. Develop a schedule and conduct BLAs with each man periodically. Again, this is the importance of having a leadership team—the chances are that one leader cannot meet with every man in the church, but you can make great strides in reaching every man as a team.

I incorporated BLAs into my state and regional ministry to meet with leaders on a monthly schedule. I have to utilize video conferencing with many, but the point is I am meeting with them and listening.

Before you go any further in, I want you to stop and pray, seeking God to give you the names of five individuals in your church with whom you can schedule a BLA. As the names come to you, go to Appendix 2 and write down each man's name, phone number, and email. Then call these men and schedule an appointment within the next month. You will be blessed, and so will the men you will meet. Also, there are some guidelines and suggestions on how to organize your BLAs in Appendix 2.

Surveys

The next method to get to know your men is doing surveys. Everybody loves surveys, don't they—NOT! But surveys can be helpful to get to know your men. Develop a simple survey. What do I mean by simple? Keep the survey to no more than five questions. Go ahead and provide several answers; the men can just check for their response and maybe put a line at the end to add anything they may desire or a comment box for electronic surveys. An example of a simple survey is in Appendix 3.

Do not ask for any personal information such as names, age, email, or phone number. Collect these through attendance records or registrations for events. If you keep the surveys anonymous, men will be more transparent about their struggles.

Surveys can inquire about interests, hobbies, activities, types of studies, struggles, missions, etc. Don't overuse surveys but conduct them two or three times a year and make sure you change the questions or subject of the survey. Otherwise, some men may recognize they have answered the questions and ignore the survey.

Doing Projects Together

Finally, as we discussed using mission opportunities as entry points for men, they can also be used to get to know the men in the church and community. This can also be accomplished by talking with your men. Develop a mission project or activity your men can sponsor through the men's ministry. While working on these projects, you will get to know your men more than you can realize.

When men are doing a comfortable project, they will begin to let their guard down and talk more freely about their lives. You may find men who are struggling in their marriage, fathering, grandfathering, careers, struggling with temptations, or a host of other struggles. Doing projects will accomplish two things: (1) the men will be ministering to the community, and (2) you will be getting to know your men.

Reach Every Man

As a church develops a vibrant ministry to men, the church needs to understand a need to ensure events, activities, and spiritual gatherings are planned to reach every man in the church and community. It takes work, and it takes a passionate leadership team to create entry points to connect with your men.

While you as a leadership team create those entry points, get to know your men by talking with them, conduct Barnabas Lunch Appointments (BLA), surveys, and doing projects. As it has been said many times in this book, Paul told the Thessalonians 2:8, "We care so much for you that we were pleased to share with you not only the Gospel of God but also our own lives." As you get to know your men, you will be showing that you care for them and that you are willing to share your life with them. Now go and create those entry points and get to know your men.

Questions to reflect on for your next step.

- What is most lacking in your church to reach men? Leadership. Finances. Promotion. Masculine Presence.

- What kind of entry points does your church conduct to help men take the next right step? If none, why not?

- What is the first step you will encourage your church to do to get to know your men? Talk with the men. Barnabas Lunch Appointments. Surveys. Doing Projects.

- What actions do you need to take?

The Call

Chapter 8
Keep the Fire Burning

The fire on the altar shall be kept burning on it; it shall not go out.
Leviticus 6:12

As I write this chapter, we are in the early days of spring. Though the days are warming, the evenings can still be a little cool. After a busy day at work or a Saturday in the yard doing the spring chores, we may like to go out after supper and sit around the fire pit and enjoy the quietness of the evening and feeling the warmth of a fire.

Fires can be mesmerizing. Sometimes, as one sits near a fire, the individual will be drawn into watching the flames flickering as the fire consumes the burning product. For some reason, as youngsters, we would always be drawn to fire, periodically throwing leaves and twigs, even paper in the fire, just to watch it catch on fire and be consumed. Every time we see a fire truck with its lights and siren blaring, we wonder where it is going and how big is the fire.

Fire has always been something that has fascinated the human heart and mind. Maybe that is why God uses fire often to describe the burning passion in his children. He used fire as a protector to prevent the Egyptian army from reaching the Israelites as they crossed the Red Sea (Ex. 14:24). God used fire to describe the working of the Holy Spirit, as we see in Acts 2 when the disciples were baptized with the Holy Spirit.

Keep the Fire Burning

In the Old Testament, when God established the priesthood's office and gave instructions for building the tabernacle, He had the Israelites build an altar where a fire was to keep burning; it was never to go out. God told the Israelites in Leviticus 6:9, "the fire of the altar shall be kept burning on it." Then He said to them two more times a little more emphatically, "The fire on the altar shall be kept burning on it; it shall not go out" (Lev. 6:12, 13).

As we return to the fire pit, the fire can help remind us to stay focused on our relationship with God and not let our fire—our passion—die. We often start those fires and don't think much about them afterward unless we focus on the fire itself. At some point, something catches our attention, and we turn our focus away from the fire, and before we know it, the fire starts to die down. Someone may say something about the dying fire, pulling our attention back for a moment as we stoke the fire or put some logs on to keep it going.

Our lives with God can be much the same. We begin our relationship with Jesus, and we are on fire for Him for a while. Then life begins to happen, and before we know it, something else has captured our attention, and the fire in our lives begins to die. At some point, God will cause something to happen to remind us we need to stoke the fire in our lives to keep it burning.

Remember how I told you about my journey at the beginning of the book of how God gained my attention with Kidney Cancer? Hopefully, it would not be as dramatic for you, but He will try and get your attention at some point.

Leader of Men

When working in men's ministry, you will need to keep the fire burning. You can do several things and some you may already be doing, but I want to emphasize the importance of each of them as you begin to be a leader of men. Now, before you say, "I am not a leader," let me say, all of us are leaders.

I was speaking with a man one time, and he told me he was not a leader. I asked him if he was a husband, he said, "Yes." I asked if he was a Father, he said, "Yes." I then reminded him that he was a leader even though he may not see himself as one by the fact he is a husband and father.

Men, understand that even if you do not lead a particular ministry in the church, you are a leader if you are a husband or a dad. Even if you are not married and a dad, there is someone who is watching you, and just for this reason, you are a leader. Every man is a leader in some way.

Do Not Neglect Devotions

I want to warn you that we can get so busy in the logistics and the ministry's busyness we can either forget or neglect (I will let you choose) our devotions. We need to be sure we spend time with God allowing Him to speak into our lives. If we don't, we will begin to feel and see its effect on our attitude. We need to keep the fire burning in our lives. I think we all can do more to encourage our men to develop an intentional and deeper understanding of our relationship with God. How to keep the fire burning?

Several years ago, while reading Leviticus, one of the items I was drawn to, though I have read it many times, was God's command to Moses and Aaron about the fire on the altar. As mentioned earlier, in Leviticus 6:12, the Lord told Moses, "The fire on the altar shall be kept burning on it; it shall not go out."

Fire Triangle

If you know anything about a fire's anatomy, you know there are three elements required for any fire to burn. The three elements that make up the fire triangle are heat, fuel, and oxygen. If you take away one of these elements, a fire can not sustain itself.[29]

First is heat. Heat must be present. Without heat, the fire will not burn. Throw some water on it, you will take away the heat, and the fire will eventually die. Second, a fire must have oxygen. Just like humans, this helps the fire to breathe and stay alive. Like us, you take away the oxygen, basically suffocating the fire, it will die. Finally, you must have fuel. It does not matter if it is wood, paper, gas, or some other product. It just needs to be a combustible product. But if you take the fuel away from the Heat and Oxygen, guess what, the fire will die. You must have all three to sustain an active fire. Firemen call this the triangle of fire. Without any one of these – heat, oxygen, fuel—taking one of the triangle sides away and the fire will die. It will not survive.

When I read the "Fire must be kept burning," I wrote in the margin of my Bible, "an example of our passion for God." Our fire must not go out, the fire that is within us. The fire that became alive in us when we surrendered to God. But let's face it, there are days when we feel this fire has gone out, or at least it is down to the embers just glowing; it is no longer a raging fire. It will not take much more for the fire to die. What do we do? What will keep this fire within us raging—burning.

Spiritual Fire Triangle

For those of us in men's ministry, we must keep the fire burning. We cannot let the fire go out. So how do we keep the fire burning? Just like the fire triangle, I have found a spiritual fire triangle for us to keep the spiritual fire burning in our lives. The spiritual fire triangle consists of (1) staying in the Word, (2) praying regularly, and (3) pouring your life into others. Then help stoke the fire by practicing the ministry of hanging out with other brothers in Christ.

Just like the fire in the Fire Pit or the Fireplace, we need three elements to keep the fire in our lives – our passion – burning for God. We need to have these disciplines in our lives active to keep that fire burning. We will look at each of these disciplines as we maintain the fire–passion–in our lives.

Read Your Bible

Think of reading your Bible as your fuel. You need to be in the Bible every day, not just when you go to church or a Bible Study. For example, when we look at the priest's duties, Leviticus 6:12 not only says they were to keep the fire burning on the altar, the verse continues to say, "The priest shall burn wood on it every morning."

Like the priest was to put wood on the altar's fire every morning, we have to put God's Word on our spiritual fire every day. Preferably it should be your first business of the day. If you have not already done so, discipline yourself to be in God's Word—Bible—every day. If you cannot make this your first act in the morning, review your daily schedule and select a time you can.

Several resources can help you develop a discipline to be in the Bible daily. I have listed a number of them in Appendix 4. If you are not already using one, pick one to start. Also, check your Bible; it may have a reading plan either in the front or back of the Bible.

Lonnie Berger, in his book *Every Man a Warrior: Helping Men Succeed in Life*, writes, "A man who stays in the Word becomes equipped for walking with God, raising children, staying married, managing money, going through hard times, enjoying his work, staying morally pure, and making his life count for something eternal." In his second letter to Timothy, Paul promised that a man in the scripture would be thoroughly equipped for every good work.

"All Scripture is God-breathed and is useful for teaching, rebuking, correcting and training in righteousness, so that the man of God may be thoroughly equipped for every good work."
2 Timothy 3:16-17 (NIV)

Depending on your reading, a devotional guide, or chapters in the Bible, you will spend about 15 to 30 minutes each time. But whatever you do, dedicate a time in the day. Get up a half-hour earlier, turn off that TV a half-hour earlier, or use your lunch break. Seek a time to do it and DO IT! Nothing will cause your fire to go out quicker than neglecting the reading of the Word, taking away the fuel of the spiritual fire. And when you read, allow it to find a place in your heart and meditate on it. "I have treasured Your word in my heart so that I may not sin against you" (Psalms 119:11).

We read in Joshua 1:8 the Lord told Joshua, "This Book of the Law shall not depart from your mouth, but you shall meditate on it day and night, so that you may be careful to do according to all that is written in it. For then you will make your way prosperous, and then you will have good success."

Reading your Bible daily is synonymous with the priest putting wood on the fire daily to keep the fire burning.

Pray

Think of prayer as your heat. Like we need to read the Bible every day, we need to be in a constant attitude of prayer and even spend time in deliberate prayer. Paul told the Thessalonians in his first letter to "Pray without ceasing" (1 Thess. 5:17). You are to always be in an attitude of prayer. To have an effective and vibrant ministry to men, you and your team need to be praying for the ministry to men regularly together.

As an individual, you need to discover your prayer room—sometimes referred to as a prayer closet—and spend time there. In Matthew 6:6, Jesus said, "When you pray, go into your room and shut the door and pray to your Father who is in secret. And your Father who sees in secret will reward you." We read in the gospels about Jesus stealing himself away to spend time in prayer (Mark 6:46; Luke 5:16), sometimes praying all night as told in Luke 6:12, "He (Jesus) went out to the mountain to pray, and all night he continued in prayer to God."

You and your team need to spend time talking and listening to God. Psalms 46:10 says, "Be still, and know that I am God." It took me a while to learn that prayer is about sharing my desires with God and listening. Hearing from God during our quiet time is an essential part of making good decisions. Hence the reason why reading the Bible and praying is such an integral part of each other.

According to K. C. Dickie, Men's Equipping Network, "The most important aspect of men praying together: they are developing intimacy with Christ. This is a game-changer. I'll go out on a limb and say that until a man finds intimacy with Christ, he'll remain lukewarm in his relationship with God." [30]

If your attitude toward prayer begins to cool, then your fire —passion—will begin to become nothing more than embers, barely hanging on.

Fellowship With Brothers

Think of fellowshipping with brothers in Christ as your oxygen. Ecclesiastes 4:9-10 tells us that, "Two are better than one, because they have a good reward for their toil. For if they fall, one will lift up his fellow." At the end of verse 10, there is a warning, "But woe to him who is alone when he falls and has not another to lift him up!" We cannot live this life alone.

Jesus sent his disciples out in twos to do ministry (Luke 10:1). The apostles had traveling companions in ministry; Peter and John in Acts 3, Barnabas and Paul (Acts 13), Barnabas and Mark, and Paul and Silas (Acts 15). All of us need brothers around us. To gather together to worship, hanging out with each other, and working together. We need others in our lives to keep us encourage and to pray with us when we begin to feel suffocated with the struggles of life.

Chapter 5 discussed the ministry of hanging out and the importance of men doing life together. The ministry of hanging out is connecting with friends and acquaintances to build relationships to encourage. The ministry of hanging out can be seen in activities such as cookouts, hunting, fishing, attending ballgames, or any number of activities where men hang out to fellowship. We need to understand that men must have other men in their lives from a Biblical perspective.

Scripture supports the thought that believers should be with and influence each other. Paul emphasized this in his letters as he used the phrase "one another" 33 times. "One another" occurs 63 times in all of the New Testament writing outside the Gospels. The New Testament writers expect believers to (1) be in proximity with one another and (2) stimulate and influence one another to become spiritually mature. We often use Hebrews 10:24-25 to encourage believers to attend church services, but these verses encourage us to be together to "stir up one another to love and good works."

Let me share a story that will help emphasize the need for men to fellowship with other men. There was a man who was active in a church. Over time, life's events started taking their toll and began to pull the man away from the church until he was not attending anymore. The pastor of the church was concerned and decided one winter evening to visit the man.

The man graciously invited the pastor into his home and offered him a chair near the fire burning in the fireplace to warm himself. After the pleasantries were said, neither the pastor nor the man said anything. At one point, the pastor got up and, with a pair of tongs, reached into the fire, pulled a piece of coal away from the fire, and then sat back down.

After a few minutes, the bright redness indicating the coal was hot began to fade to the point it did not appear to be hot anymore. At that point, the pastor took the tongs, picked up the coal, and put it back in the fire. Shortly afterward, the coal was red hot again.

After a few more minutes, the pastor said he needed to take his leave and continue with his tasks for the day. The man responded to the pastor by thanking him for the sermon, and he would be in church the following Sunday.

> *We need to have brothers in our lives to encourage us in our walk with Christ and keep the fire burning.*

The moral of the story is that we may think we can do Christian life alone, but we cannot. We need to have brothers in our lives to encourage us in our walk with Christ and keep the fire burning.

Pour Your Life Into Others

Several times in this book, you have read the verse from 1 Thessalonians 2:8, "Being affectionately desirous of you, we were ready to share with you not only the gospel of God but also our own selves, because you had become very dear to us." As a leader of men, other than reading the Bible and praying, nothing will encourage you more and keep your fire burning than pouring your life into other men.

During your prayer time, being still and listening to God, ask for God to give you a name to pour your life into. Could be one of the men you will contact as you begin your BLA Ministry.

Summary

This is the Spiritual Fire Triangle; Read Your Bible (fuel), Pray (heat), and Fellowship With Brothers (oxygen). Then as a bonus, pour your life into others. You must keep the fire burning; it must not go out. If your fire is dying and it is just the embers' slight glow or has gone out completely, examine yourself like we are told to do in Lamentation 3:40. "Let us test and examine our ways." You may find out that one of these disciplines is missing from your life. If one is, put it back into the mix to keep the fire burning—activate the fire again.

The Call

Questions *to reflect on for your next step.*

- Examine yourself like told to do in Lamentation 3:40. "Let us test and examine our ways." Do you see anything you need to change about reading your Bible, prayer, or fellowship?

- What do you need to change or start doing? Explain.

- Do you have a man in your life that you can share your success and failures and pray with you? If not, pray about asking for someone and write their name here to approach them about being a prayer partner. _____

- What actions do you need to take?

Epilogue

Throughout this book, I have tried to help you understand the need to take ministering to men seriously. Men need other men in their lives. Men need men who will disciple and mentor them to be the men God created them to be. Men need men who can be transparent, allowing other men to speak encouragement into their lives. Men are in a battle, a Battle for Men's Souls.

Churches serious about ministering to men will seek a leader who has a passion and burden to speak into a man's life. The church will seek a leader called to be a men's leader, maybe even a men's pastor. They will develop a leadership team and train that team, so when the men's leader is called to another position, there will be a man ready to step into that leader's role.

The Call

When I began to minister to men, I did not have a clue what to do. It wasn't until God put men in my life to disciple and mentor me did I realize the responsibility associated with being a leader of men. In addition, all these mentors helped me understand the resources available. I pray you will find such a mentor.

If you are unsure where to start, a great place is to begin conducting Barnabas Lunch Appointments (BLA) with the men you wrote down in Appendix 2 from Chapter 7. If you didn't do that, do it now. I challenge you to stop and pray right now for God to reveal five men for you to reach out to and schedule a BLA. As those names come to you, go to Appendix 2 and write down their names, phone numbers, and emails. Then call one of them and schedule your first BLA. You will be blessed, and so will they.

I pray your church will begin to target their men in everything they do. I pray they will take a serious look at the budget for the ministry to men. I pray your church will promote the ministry as much as they do other ministries. I pray they will consider developing areas in the church that reflect a man-friendly environment. I pray you will heed the words of my mentor Jeff Kisiah as he told me more than once, "You need to be intentional in your relationship with men, you need to create multiple entry points for them to connect with the ministry, and you need to get to know your men."

I pray this book has given you some ideas and encouraged you to not only go and make disciples but to reach the men in your church and surrounding community. As you develop an effective and vibrant ministry to men in your church, then we will be working together,

To the challenge and adventure to disciple every man.

The Call

Appendix 1
The Roman Road

Romans 3:23
For all have sinned and fall short of the glory of God

Romans 5:8
But God demonstrates His own love toward us, in that while we were yet sinners, Christ died for us.

Romans 6:23
For the wages of sin is death, but the free gift of God is eternal life in Christ Jesus our Lord.

The Call

Romans 10:9-10
If you confess with your mouth Jesus as Lord, and believe in your heart that God raised Him from the dead, you will be saved; for with the heart a person believes, resulting in righteousness, and with the mouth he confesses, resulting in salvation.

Romans 10:13
"WHOEVER WILL CALL ON THE NAME OF THE LORD WILL BE SAVED."

Sinners Prayer for Forgiveness:
Dear God, I know I am a sinner. I know my sin deserves to be punished. I believe that Jesus is the Son of God, who died for me and rose from the grave. I want to turn from my sin and trust Jesus Christ alone as my Savior. Thank you for the forgiveness and for everlasting life I can now have through faith in Jesus. In Jesus' name. Amen.

Now go and tell someone in your church what you have done. If you do not have a church, you can reach out to me at capefearmen@gmail.com. But tell someone.

A Journey Into Men's Ministry

Appendix 2

Barnabas Lunch Appointments (BLA)**

List five men to reach out to schedule a BLA

Name	Phone	Email

The Call

A Barnabas Lunch Appointment is an opportunity for you as a leader to intentionally spend time with men in a one-on-one interaction. The goal of these meetings is to provide a safe environment where they can freely "raise the window shade."

Here's how to use this strategy to increase your impact on men's lives.

1. Choose one day a week (or more) and reserve your lunchtime (or breakfast/supper) for your Barnabas Lunch Appointment.
2. Make a list of men you would like to target. For a pastor, it may be every man in the church. For a lay leader, it may be men in your Sunday School class or small group.
3. Send emails or call and reserve a lunch appointment on your BLA day. Over time, you will find men contacting you for the opportunity.
4. Be ready with some questions or topics to guide the discussion forward. You don't want to fill your whole time with surface matters. Instead, take advantage and talk about real-life issues. Here are a few suggestions:
   - For a man who needs Christ—What brings you fulfillment in life?
   - For a cultural Christian—Some guys just hit their spiritual "time clock" on Sunday morning. How has Jesus impacted the rest of your life?

- For all types of men—Do you have some "foxhole friends," and what impact are they having on your spiritual journey?

5. Close the time together in a private location with prayerful support. If you can, always meet at the same location and choose a spot outside to pray—perhaps under a specific tree. As you continue to meet the men, that will become a special place for you and the men you are discipling. In my times of intercession, I often pray for God to provide three things in a man's life.

   - A Rock—to stand on.
   - A Brook—to drink from.
   - A Tree—to be shaded by.

Keep a journal of your meetings to track a man's progress on his spiritual journey and see what God is doing over time. Use a spreadsheet like this one. It's helpful as a prayer guide, ministry review, record for your next BLA, and reminder of God's hand in these men's lives.

See Chart on the Next Page

The Call

Day	Date	Time	Appointment	Location	Notes/Follow-up/Resources
Mon	Jan 30	12:00 pm	Maury T,	Island's	Provided copy of *The Case for Christ*
Wed	Feb 1	11:00 am	Mike M.	McAlister	Followed up his EMAW studies
Thur.	Feb 2	12:30 pm	John E.	Sawmill	Encourage as a MDL

Here are some ministry objectives for this weekly "BLA Tour:"

- Intentionality—Men need to see this principle put into practice regularly!
- Accessibility—Move beyond the standard group interaction to these 1-1 times.
- Coachability—Discern where a man is on the Journey to Biblical Manhood.
- Sustainability—Strive to help "rekindle the flame" in a man's spiritual life.

The ministry of "hanging out" is the essence of 1-1 discipleship.—Jeff Kisiah

**Adapted from the ministry and teaching of my mentor Pastor Jeff "Coach K" Kisiah.

Appendix 3
Example of a Simple Survey

What are your Hobbies/Interests?
_____
_____
_____

Spiritual Journey

How would you classify yourself currently (check any that apply)?
___ Minimal interest in Christianity
___ Inquiring about spiritual matters

The Call

___ New Believer in Christ
___ Desiring growth towards greater spiritual maturity
___ On the path to Biblical Manhood
___ Aspiring Leader, as God allows
___ Hurting Man (in a season of suffering)
___ Other: _____

Personal Development

Check any/all of these opportunities that might interest you:
___ Men's Conference
___ Discipleship Group
___ Community Outreach
___ Disaster Relief
___ Prayer Group
___ Men's Leadership Team
___ Mission Trip
___ Ministry Volunteer (Youth / Children / Worship / Guest Services)
___ Other: _____

Social Involvement

___ Sports (League Play, Group Tickets, TV Viewing Parties, etc.)
___ Outdoors (Hiking, Camping, Fishing, Hunting, Archery, etc.)
___ Indoors, (Bowling, Billiards, Ping Pong, Arcade, etc.)
___ Cars (Auto Fairs, Racing Events, etc.)
___ Other: _____

Additional Comments

_____
_____
_____

The Call

Appendix 4
Resources

These are resources to help you develop a discipline of reading the Bible regularly and spending time in prayer. Developing a Quiet Time is essential for all men as they grow spiritually in Christ.

- Finding Treasures in the Psalms Daily Devotion. Author: Charles Hall
- My Utmost for His Highest. Author: Oswell Chambers
- One Year Bible
- Open Windows Devotional Guide
- Stand Firm Day by Day: Let Nothing Move You – Walk thru the Bible
- Stand Firm Magazine: God's Challenge for Today's Man

The Call

- Stand Strong – 365 Devotions for Men by Men
- The Men's Bible, National Coalition of Ministering to Men

Endnotes

1. Dr. Bill Bennett. Handbook For Mentoring Men for the Master. New Hanover Printing and Publishing. Wilmington. p.159
2. Dr. Bill Bennett. Handbook For Mentoring Men for the Master. New Hanover Printing and Publishing. Wilmington. p.160
3. You Raise me Up. Song written by Brendan Graham. Lyrics pulled from website St Lyrics, https://www.stlyrics.com/lyrics/celticwoman/youraisemeup.htm
4. U.S. Church Membership Down Sharply in Past Two Decades. Gallop Poll Article. https://news.gallup.com/poll/248837/church-membership-down-sharply-past-two-decades.aspx. 2019
5. The State of The Church. Barna Research Article. https://www.barna.com/research/state-church-2016/. 2016
6. Wiersbe's Expository Outlines on the New Testament, Warren Wiersbe, 1992, SP Publications, p36

7. Ray Pritchard. What Happened To Judas? Article in Crosswalk. https://www.crosswalk.com/church/pastors-or-leadership/what-happened-to-judas-11532302.html. 2007.

8. David Jeremiah. Agents of the Apocalypse: A Riveting Look at the Key Players of the End Times (p. 248). Tyndale House Publishers, Inc.. Kindle Edition.

9. Cedarmont Kids – O Be Careful, Little Eyes Lyrics, https://www.metrolyrics.com/o-be-careful-little-eyes-lyrics-cedarmont-kids.html, © 2021 Metrolyrics, A Red Ventures Company. All Rights Reserved.

10. James Emery White. Eight Strategic Decisions. Article on Crosswalk website. https://www.crosswalk.com/blogs/dr-james-emery-white/decisions-eight-strategic-strategies.html. 2017

11. Patrick Morley, David Delk, and Brett Clemmer. No Man Left Behind: How to Build and Sustain a Thriving Disciple-Making Ministry for Every Man in Your Church. Moody Publishers. Chicago. 2006. Pg. 83.

12. Thompson, Michael. The Heart of a Warrior: Before You Can Become the Warrior, You Must Become the Beloved Son (p. 12). Heart & Life Publishers. Kindle Edition.

13. Richard Foster. Celebration of Discipline. 25th Anniv. Ed. New York. Harper Collins. 1988. Pg. 107.

14. https://churchformen.com/men-and-church/

15. Merriam-Webster On-line Dictionary, https://www.merriam-webster.com/dictionary/discipling, 2021 Merriam-Webster, Incorporated

16. Merriam-Webster On-line Dictionary, https://www.merriam-webster.com/dictionary/disciple, 2021 Merriam-Webster, Incorporated

17. Merriam-Webster On-line Dictionary, https://www.merriam-webster.com/dictionary/-ing, 2021 Merriam-Webster, Incorporate

18. Merriam-Webster On-line Dictionary, https://www.merriam-webster.com/dictionary/mentor, 2021 Merriam-Webster, Incorporated
19. Robert Young. Young's Analytical Concordance. Associated Publishers and Authors Inc. Grand Rapids
20. The Strongest NASB Exhaustive Concordance. Zondervan. LaHabra. 1981
21. Lonnie Berger. Every Man a Warrior: Helping Men Succeed In Life – Walking With God. Every Man A Warrior. Omaha. 2014. Pg. 16.
22. Dale Forhand. Often Told Rarely Trained: Becoming the man you've always been told to be. Stained Glass Ministries. Birmingham. 2013. Pg. 13.
23. Campbell, Regi. Mentor Like Jesus: His Radical Approach to Building the Church. RM Press. Kindle Edition.
24. Kisiah, Jeff. http://intentionalway.org/what-is/
25. Gary Yagel. Got Your Back: Helping Christian Men Forge The Brotherhood Connections They Need. Xulon Press. 2015. Pg. 5.
26. Various Authors. How To Disciple Men. National Coalition of Ministries to Men. Broadstreet Publishing. Racine. 2017. Pg. 33.
27. Ibid. pg. 22.
28. Patrick Morley, David Delk, and Brett Clemmer. No Man Left Behind: How to Build and Sustain a Thriving Disciple-Making Ministry for Every Man in Your Church. Moody Publishers. Chicago. 2006. Pg. 130.
29. Article. Fire Triangle: Three Necessary Ingrdients of Fire. Ferdindand Furer. https://spectrumlocalnews.com/tx/san-antonio/weather/2020/10/30/fire-triangle#:~:text=Air%20is%20made%2Dup%20of,%2C%20fires%20won't%20burn. 2020
30. Various Authors. How To Disciple Men. National Coalition of Ministries to Men. Broadstreet Publishing. Racine. 2017. Pg 167.

The Call

Author: Mike Sandlin

Mike has always had a passion for reaching men for Christ; but, after being diagnosed with Renal Cell Carcinoma (Kidney Cancer) in December 2006, the reality of the need to impact men's lives became paramount. Since then, Mike has led Men Bible Studies and Discipleship Groups to encourage men in their walk with Christ. He speaks at men's groups regularly and spends hours just talking to men about their spiritual walk. His life verse comes from 1 Thessalonians 2:8, *"So, being affectionately desirous of you, we were ready to share with you not only the gospel of God but also our own selves, because you had become very dear to us."* The key here is to share or pour his life into others.

Mike earned his bachelor's degree in Business Administration from the University of Mount Olive in Mount Olive, NC. His concentration was in Management and Organizational Development. Mike retired from Duke Energy in March 2016 after 42 years. He established and led teams performing incident investigations and developing and overseeing projects for Duke Energy. In the last several years of service, Mike was responsible for overseeing the Corrective Action and Human Performance Improvements for Duke Energy's Nuclear Division Reactor Services group.

Mike and Joanne have been married for 46 years and live in Hampstead, NC. They have two children and two grandchildren. He and his wife are active members of Scotts Hill Baptist Church in Wilmington, NC, where he teaches a Sunday morning class and serves as an Elder. In addition, Mike was a Field Representative for Man in the Mirror for four years. He currently serves with the Cape Fear Network of Baptist Churches as a Men's Ministry Consultant and as the NC Baptist on Mission Men's Ministry State Coordinator. Mike is also a member of the National Coalition of Ministries to Men and is part of the Iron Sharpens Iron National Men's Equipping Conference Network.

You can find out more about Mike and his ministry by going to www.CapeFearMen.net.

Follow Mike and Cape Fear Men on Facebook @capefearmen and on his podcasts.

Intentional Conversations with Mike Sandlin. Mike interviews men's ministry leaders providing information on resources available for men from around the world. Intentional Conversations with Mike Sandlin is a Men's Ministy Leader Interviewing Leaders In Men's Ministry.

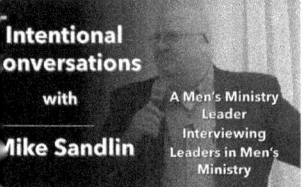

Men's Ministry Moments. These are approximately five minutes episodes providing insights, ideas, and information on ministering to men.

You can find both of these on iTunes, Spotify, iHeart, YouTube and most other podcast sites. Be sure follow both of these podcasts so you can receive the latest episodes.

www.ingramcontent.com/pod-product-compliance
Lightning Source LLC
Chambersburg PA
CBHW062223080426
42734CB00010B/2005